Adventures with the SANTA FE TRAIL

Revised edition

An activity book for kids and teachers

By Dave Webb

Illustrated by Phillip R. Buntin

Dr. Leo E. Oliva
Historical consultant

Kansas Heritage Center
Dodge City, Kansas

Adventures with the Santa Fe Trail

The jingling ox chains and mule harnesses are silent, the creaking wagon wheels roll no more—but over a century after the Santa Fe Trail was abandoned, there is still interest in this historic road between Missouri and New Mexico. As Trail scholar Marc Simmons has said, "The Santa Fe Trail lives on!"

This activity book is designed to help kids and teachers study different aspects of the Trail. Each section includes an information article along with one or more related activity pages. Activities are based on a variety of skills and can be completed by individuals or groups, depending on students' abilities and grade levels. For suggestions on adapting some activities to different levels, and for study projects, see "Digging deeper" (pages 68–71).

Glossary words are highlighted one or more times in the text and are defined in "Trail terms" (pages 60–61).

ISBN 1-882404-05-X
Kansas Heritage Center
P.O. Box 1207
Dodge City, Kansas 67801-1207

Suggested books (page 58 and elsewhere) followed by a **P** are in print. Titles marked with a star* are suitable for younger readers.

These people graciously provided information for this book, or helped in its preparation: artist Phillip R. Buntin; Trail scholars Leo E. Oliva, Mark L. Gardner, Marc Simmons; Laurel Drew, Albuquerque Public Library; Patricia Michaelis, Robert Knecht, and Thomas Witty, Kansas State Historical Society; George Elmore, Fort Larned National Historic Site; Bob Moore, Jefferson National Expansion Memorial; Alejendra Aldred, Bent's Old Fort National Historic Site; Pat O'Brien, Denver Service Center, National Park Service; Deana Reimer, USD 443 ESL director, Dodge City; Bill Bunyan and his fifth grade class, Lincoln Elementary School, Dodge City; Joyce Puderbaugh and her fifth grade class, Protection Elementary School, Protection, Kansas; and the staff of the Kansas Heritage Center: Noel Ary, director; Betty Braddock, retired director; Jeanie Covalt, librarian; and Barbara Vincent, secretary. Printed by Spearville News, Incorporated, Spearville, Kansas.

Contents copyright © 1993, reprinted 1995. An individual purchaser may reproduce materials in this activity book for personal or classroom use only. The purchase of this book does not entitle reproduction of any part for an entire school, district, or system. Such use is strictly prohibited.

The Santa Fe National Historic Trail logo on pages 11 and 56 appears with the permission of the National Park Service.

Table of contents

A trail into history
- 4 *An overview of the Santa Fe Trail*
- 7 Adventure, *told by Trail voices*
- 8 Francis X. Aubry, *Trail traveler biography*
- 9 Marion Russell, *Trail traveler biography*
- 10 The Trail, 1610–1848, *timeline activity*
- 11 The Trail, 1849–1987, *timeline activity*
- 12 Flags over the Trail, *flag identification activity*
- 13 ¿Habla usted español? *vocabulary activity*

Routes to Santa Fe
- 14 *Roads caravans took to Santa Fe*
- 16 "Kit" Carson, *Trail traveler biography*
- 17 "Buffalo Bill" and "Lissie" Mathewson, *Trail travelers biography*
- 18 William Bent, *Trail traveler biography*
- 19 Mile after mile with Josiah Gregg, *math activity*
- 20 Tracking the Trail, *mapping activity*
- 25 Mystery map, *mapping activity*

Barrels, bundles, bales
- 26 *Cargoes hauled on the Trail*
- 27 Antonio José Chávez, *Trail traveler biography*
- 28 Mariano Yrissarri's bill of goods, *math activity*
- 29 Josiah Gregg's graphs, *graphing activity*
- 30 J.J. Webb's puzzling list, *puzzle activity*
- 31 J.J. Webb's trade items, *categorizing activity*

Hard work, long hours
- 32 *Jobs on a wagon train*
- 33 Alexander Majors, *Trail traveler biography*
- 34 Robert Wright, *Trail traveler biography*
- 35 Trail work and wages, *math and charting activity*
- 36 Bosses, teamsters, herders, *outlining activity*

On the march
- 37 *A typical day on the Santa Fe Trail*
- 38 Weather, *told by Trail voices*
- 39 Susan Magoffin, *Trail traveler biography*
- 40 A long day on the Trail, *sequencing activity*

A choice: mules or oxen
- 41 *Draft animals used on the Trail*
- 42 Wheelers, leaders, pointers, *diagramming activity*
- 43 Spans of mules—or yokes of oxen? *math and charting activity*

Conestogas, J. Murphys
- 44 *Popular Santa Fe Trail wagons*
- 45 Trail schooner, *diagramming activity*

Conflicts on the Trail
- 46 *Trail trouble and the forts built to prevent it*
- 49 Indians, *told by Trail voices*
- 50 Franz and Ernestine Huning, *Trail travelers biography*
- 51 Little Raven, *Trail traveler biography*
- 52 Scouting the Trail forts, *mapping activity*
- 53 Trail forts, 1808–1900, *timeline activity*
- 54 Conflicting stories, *discussion activity*

Trail resources and review
- 56 Trail places, *historic sites and museums to visit*
- 57 Trail Times, *creative writing activity*
- 58 Trail books, *books to read*
- 59 Bookin' on down the Trail, *book report activity*
- 60 Trail terms, *glossary of Trail words*
- 62 Trail terms practice, *vocabulary activity*
- 63 Conestoga crossword, *puzzle activity*
- 64 A table of Trail travelers, *charting activity*
- 65 Quick quiz, *review activity*
- 66 Trail review, *review activity*
- 68 Digging deeper, *suggestions for Trail projects*
- 72 Answer keys

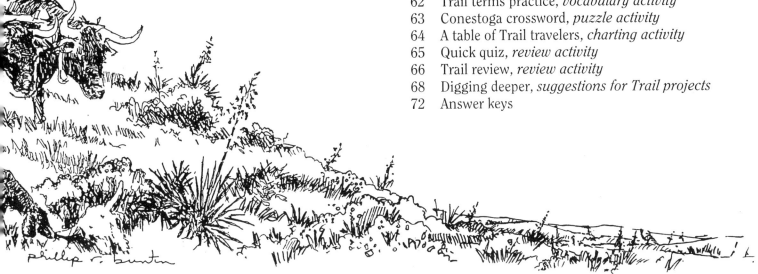

A trail into history

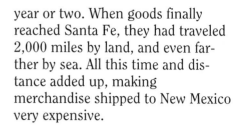

The Santa Fe Trail: For daring men like Francis X. Aubry it was a road to fortune and adventure. For courageous women like Marion Sloan Russell it was a highway along which to build a home. For Western legends like "Kit" Carson it was a route to fame. And for you, it can be a trail into history.

More than a century after it closed, you can still experience the excitement of the Santa Fe Trail. It's all there—in books, maps, museums, and Trail sites—if you let history live in your imagination.

The Santa Fe Trail is the oldest overland road across the Great Plains. It began as a **commerce** route between the United States and Mexico, but it became much more. During six busy decades, the trail to Santa Fe was a supply line for the U.S. Army, a mail route, and a road over which adventurers, gold-seekers, settlers, and others traveled to the West.

The **Trail** was also a cultural link between nations: Mexico and its Old World ideas of colonial empires—America, an expanding New World democracy—and the Plains Indians, an independent people caught in between. While the road to Santa Fe unfortunately helped end the Indians' traditional cultures, it created ties between the Spanish and American cultures that still remain.

An isolated city

The Trail's story begins with the little city of Santa Fe, founded in 1610 as the capital of Spanish New Mexico. For over two hundred years, Santa Fe was almost isolated from the rest of the world. The large cities of Mexico were far to the south. Spain jealously protected its colony's borders, and strict laws made it difficult for outsiders to visit. Other Spanish laws made it illegal for New Mexicans to manufacture goods or trade with foreigners.

As a result, the citizens of Santa Fe had only one way to get supplies: by ships from Spain to the Mexican port of Veracruz, then by wagons to Mexico City and Chihuahua. Pack mules and carts traveled the 600 miles on to Santa Fe, but that part of the trip was made only once every year or two. When goods finally reached Santa Fe, they had traveled 2,000 miles by land, and even farther by sea. All this time and distance added up, making merchandise shipped to New Mexico very expensive.

By the early 1800s, American settlements had pushed west, nearer to Santa Fe. But most U.S. citizens who tried to visit New Mexico were not welcomed. In 1807, Lieutenant Zebulon Pike and a group of men exploring part of America's new Louisiana Purchase lands were arrested by Spanish soldiers.

When Pike was released, he returned to the United States with stories of the incredible prices New Mexicans were willing to pay for cloth and simple hardware items. Hearing this news, several Frenchmen, Americans, and others tried to trade in New Mexico.

A few were successful, slipping in and out of Spanish territory without being arrested. But most, like Robert McKnight and James Baird in 1812, were put in jail or had their merchandise taken away. (Some of those in the McKnight-Baird party were held in Chihuahua until 1821.)

Revolution opens the way

The situation changed when, after 11 years of trying, the Mexican people **revolted** against Spain in 1821. Once free of colonial rule, they set up a new government and threw out the old Spanish laws against foreign trade. Then, almost before news of the Mexican Revolution had time to reach the United States, American traders appeared in Santa Fe.

The first party to arrive was led by William Becknell. He, along with five men and several packhorses, had set out from Franklin, Missouri, on the first of September, 1821. In a newspaper announcement before they left, Becknell said he planned to trade with Indians, trap for furs, and catch wild horses along the Arkansas River. What he didn't say was that he was deep in debt and desperately needed cash.

That may have been the reason Becknell and his group dared to leave the Arkansas at the edge of the mountains and travel south into what had been forbidden Spanish territory. Becknell's risk paid off near the village of San Miguel. There he and his men met a party of Mexican soldiers who greeted the Americans as guests—not trespassers.

Encouraged, the Missourians traveled on to Santa Fe and entered the city on November 16. After being welcomed by Governor Facundo Melgares they soon sold their trade goods. With a profit of silver coins, mules, and blankets, they returned to Franklin in January 1822.

Two weeks after Becknell and his group reached Santa Fe, James McKnight, Thomas James, and nine others arrived with a cargo of cloth to sell. Their profits were not as large as Becknell's, but they found McKnight's brother Robert, who had been missing since his 1812 trip to New Mexico. And so, after two centuries of isolation, Santa Fe was open to outsiders.

A busy but dangerous trail

In the spring of 1822 Becknell returned to New Mexico with cloth, **dry goods**, hardware, and other trade items. His second trip was perhaps as important as his first, for he carried goods in three wagons—the first wagons ever used on the Trail. And, when he crossed the Arkansas River and headed southwest toward the Cimarron River, he pioneered parts of the **Cimarron Route**—the road most Santa Fe traders used until the mid 1860s. For his efforts, Becknell has been called the Father of the Santa Fe Trail.

Trade between American merchants and New Mexicans grew rapidly. However, traders quickly discovered that the Trail could be dangerous. Stampedes like one witnessed by Robert Wright in 1862 injured men and livestock, damaged merchandise, and delayed **caravans**. Crossing streams could be hazardous, too, as Susan Magoffin learned in 1846.

Traders often traveled in the summer when the scorching sun and hot winds dried up water holes and wore down **draft animals** and men. In the early spring or late fall, Trail caravans sometimes ran into surprise blizzards. One trader lost 400 out of 750 mules in a sudden snowstorm in 1840. In 1848 over 800 oxen on a U.S. government train froze to death in icy weather.

In 1822, James Baird and Samuel Chambers were caught in a fall blizzard west of where Dodge City is located today. Most of their pack animals died, and the men spent the winter camped along the Arkansas River. The next spring, they dug pits in the side of a nearby hill, stored their trade goods inside, and traveled to Taos to buy more animals. (The remains of their storage pits were known as the **Caches**, a Trail landmark for many years.)

At war

When some in the unlucky Baird and Chambers party returned to collect their stored goods the next summer, they were attacked by Indians—another hazard on the Trail. However, some seasons were less dangerous than others. During part of the 1830s, few wagon trains were bothered by Indians; yet almost every train was attacked in 1847. Several times, beginning in 1829, American soldiers were sent along to protect trade caravans.

Over the years, the U.S. government built a line of forts along the Trail. Indian leaders like Little Raven spoke out for peace, and some tribes signed peace treaties. But even so, fighting continued. Trader Franz and Ernestine Huning's relatives who were killed in central Kansas in 1867 were just two of the many travelers—and Indians—who died in bloodshed along the road.

And conflicts between traders and tribes were not the only trouble on the Trail. In the 1840s, the Republic of Texas claimed land west to the Rio Grande, including Santa Fe. This caused a border conflict that brewed for several years. In 1841 Mexican troops arrested some Texans headed to Santa Fe. Two years later, Texas raiders known as "Texians" patrolled the Trail in search of Mexican traders to rob. At the same time, some Texas supporters from Missouri murdered merchant Antonio José Chávez on the Trail and stole the gold, cash, and furs with which he had planned to buy trade goods.

In 1846 the United States entered the conflict by declaring war on Mexico. The Trail became a road of

conquest when Colonel Stephen Watts Kearny led the first of over 1,600 troops out of Fort Leavenworth that spring. During the summer, forces gathered at **Bent's Fort**, a trading post on the **Mountain Route** built by Indian trader William Bent and his brothers.

That August, Kearny's Army of the West crossed Raton Pass and easily took control of Santa Fe. When the Mexican War ended in 1848, Santa Fe was a part of new American territory that stretched to the Pacific. Traffic on the Trail remained heavy as the U.S. Army shipped tons of supplies to new forts in the West.

In the 1860s the Civil War spilled onto the Trail. Confederate troops invaded New Mexico and took control of Santa Fe in March 1862. Two weeks later, Union soldiers surprised Confederates in Apache Canyon, on the Trail just east of Santa Fe. The battle that followed—and another clash at nearby Glorieta Pass two days later—helped drive the invaders back into Texas. Soon Santa Fe and all of New Mexico were again under U.S. control.

Others use the Trail

After gold was discovered in California in 1848, several thousand eager Forty-Niners used the Trail on their way to the gold fields. More hopeful miners traveled the Trail a decade later during the Colorado gold rush.

Monthly U.S. mail service between Santa Fe and Independence began in 1849. A few years later the trips were increased to weekly, with daily service by 1860. Passengers were carried, too. Travelers in 1857 paid top prices—$125 in the summer and $150 in the winter—for a rough trip in a small wagon. Between Council Grove and settlements in New Mexico, passengers often slept on the open prairie. Later, stage stations were added along the route, but some were only crude **dugouts**.

As stage lines and other traffic increased, **road ranches**, or trading ranches, were built along the Trail. Between the 1850s and 1870s there were at least nine road ranches in central Kansas, and others farther west. Most offered sleeping space for travelers, a corral for livestock, and a trading post for Indians and Trail travelers. The ranches were often run by young men, but at least one Kansas ranch was managed by a husband and wife—William "Buffalo Bill" and "Lissie" Mathewson.

During and after the Civil War, Trail traffic set new records. From May to November 1865, an amazing parade passed over a toll bridge at Council Grove: 4,472 wagons, 5,197 men, 1,267 horses, 6,452 mules, 38,281 oxen, 112 carriages, and 13,056 tons of freight.

The next year, over 5,000 wagons carried $40 million worth of goods to New Mexico. By that time, most merchandise moved in fleets of wagons owned by large freighting companies like the firm run by Alexander Majors

From ruts to rails

The Santa Fe Trail was a wagon road for almost 60 years. But the steady stream of men, animals, and vehicles that began with William Becknell's small caravan in 1822 dwindled to a trickle as new trails made of steel were laid into New Mexico.

As railroads built westward, traders shipped goods to the last town on the line and loaded their wagons there. One locomotive could pull freight cars holding the cargo of many large wagons, making it faster and cheaper to haul freight by rail than by trail.

By June 1867 the Union Pacific Railroad, Eastern Division, had reached Ellsworth, Kansas. Wagons left the **railhead** there and headed southwest to the Arkansas River where they followed the original Trail. Caravans left from Hays the next year. When the Union Pacific built into Colorado, traders abandoned the Kansas sections of the Trail to military traffic and mail coaches.

The Atchison, Topeka, and Santa Fe Railroad eventually replaced the Trail in western Kansas, Colorado, and New Mexico. In places, AT&SF crews laid rails directly over wagon ruts. The track reached Dodge City in the fall of 1872, and the Colorado border that winter. Las Animas, Colorado, was the end of the line in 1875. By late 1878 trains were running over parts of "Uncle Dick" Wootton's old **toll road** across Raton Pass. And then, on February 9, 1880, the first AT&SF train steamed into Santa Fe—ending forever the wagon days of the Santa Fe Trail.

Trail VOICES

Adventure

Josiah Gregg traveled the Santa Fe Trail in the 1830s. On his first trip, he was a sickly young bookkeeper hoping to improve his poor health in the West. By his final trip, he was a successful trader who loved the adventure of "prairie life." In 1844 Josiah wrote about the Santa Fe trade. His book, *Commerce of the Prairies* (University of Oklahoma Press reprint, 1990) P, is still one of the best sources for Trail information. Here is how Gregg described the excitement of a caravan leaving Council Grove, and later, its arrival in Santa Fe:

"'All's set!' is finally heard from some teamster—'All's set,' is directly responded from every quarter. 'Stretch out!' immediately [shouts] the captain. Then, the 'heps!' of drivers—the cracking of whips—the trampling of feet—the occasional creak of wheels—the rumbling of wagons—form a new scene of exquisite confusion.... 'Fall in!' is heard from head-quarters, and the wagons are forthwith strung out upon the long inclined plain, which stretches to the heights beyond Council Grove....

"The arrival [in Santa Fe] produced a great deal of bustle and excitement among the natives. '*Los Americanos!*'—'*Los carros!*'—'*La entrada de la caravana!*' were to be heard in every direction; and crowds of women and boys flocked around....

"The wagoners [drivers] were by no means free from excitement on this occasion.... They were prepared, with clean faces, sleek combed hair, and their choicest Sunday suit, to meet the 'fair eyes' of glistening black that were sure to stare at them as they passed. [And] each wagoner must tie a bran new 'cracker' to the lash of his whip; for, on driving through the streets and the *plaza pública*, every one strives to outvie his comrades in the dexterity with which he flourishes this favorite badge of authority."

In the summer of 1864, 16-year-old George Vanderwalker worked as a bullwhacker on a caravan from Fort Leavenworth to Fort Union. In *On the Santa Fe Trail*, edited by Marc Simmons (University Press of Kansas, 1986) P, Vanderwalker remembered a Trail stampede along the Arkansas River:

"At the crossing, and just previous to making camp, we had a stampede, caused by the night herder, who was riding in a wagon near the rear of the train, shaking his blankets. His team commenced running and excited the others....

"The cattle never quit going until they piled themselves into such a heap they could get no farther. There were steers with broken legs, besides scattered freight and damaged wagons, and it took a good week's work mending our wagon breaks with rawhides and such material as we had with us in the train, and replenishing our lost stock ... before we were able to continue our journey.

"Two of the wagons were [left] without any rear wheels ... and in this manner they [were dragged on poles] to Fort Union, New Mexico."

Matt Field, a young actor and writer, traveled to Santa Fe in 1839. In *Matt Field on the Santa Fe Trail*, edited by John E. Sunder (University of Oklahoma Press reprint, 1995) P, he described dragging wagons over rugged Raton Pass on the Mountain Route:

"The banks [of one stream] were so steep that the wagons were obliged to be roped around the trees and lowered, and again upon the opposite side a half a day was consumed in dragging the loaded vehicles up the precipitous ascent. One of the wagons was half way up the ascent when the tongue and traces broke and the enormous vehicle[,] with its heavy and closely packed contents, rushed back into the creek.

"One man flung himself upon his face, seeming to gather himself almost into nothing with terror, as he shrunk between the four wheels, and the wagon darted over his head. He was in the act of placing a stone behind one of the wheels to prevent the wagon from slipping back, when the accident occurred, and the rapidity of his action alone saved his life. Another fellow was straining at a wheel to assist it forward, and he was saved by suddenly seizing the root of a tree. Though only slightly hurt, his clothes were nearly all torn from him...."

Teenaged Lewis H. Garrard had adventures up and down the Trail in 1846 and 1847, and then wrote of them in *Wah-to-yah and the Taos Trail* (University of Oklahoma Press reprint, 1955) P. Garrard celebrated a birthday while at Fort Mann:

"[June 15] was my eighteenth birthday. Quite a different one from the last—then at home, and nothing particular to do but to cast enervated [uninterested] glances at dull books—here, ... surrounded by the most hostile Indians on the continent, my scalp in danger of sudden hoisting on some yelling Camanche's lancepoint—my body drenched by the frequent night rains. Well! there is something refreshing in variety, and the comforts of civilization will be better appreciated when regained."

Trail TRAVELER

Francis X. Aubry

Of all those who traveled the Santa Fe Trail, perhaps no one had more exciting adventures than a young trader named Francis X. Aubry. An amazing speed record he set on the Trail has never been broken.

Aubry was born in Quebec, Canada, in 1824. At the age of 19, he left his home to help support his family. In St. Louis, the French-speaking Canadian found work as a clerk and quickly learned English.

Eager trader

Just before the start of the Mexican War in 1846, he joined a wagon train to Santa Fe. Young Aubry carried his own goods, purchased on credit. In New Mexico, he sold everything within three weeks and made several thousand dollars in profit.

The next spring, Francis borrowed money and led his own wagons to Santa Fe. He sold all of his goods in one week, returned to Missouri, and decided to take another **caravan** to New Mexico that same season. Most traders tried only one trip a year, but Aubry and his wagons made the second journey in five weeks. He was back in Santa Fe by October.

Then, in December, he announced he would make an "expeditious" trip to Missouri. The 23-year-old wanted to prove it was possible to take three caravans to Santa Fe in a year.

When he arrived in Independence on January 5, 1848, just 14 days had passed. During the trip he had ten mules stolen by Mexican bandits, was delayed half a day by Indians, and waited half a day during a snowstorm. He killed three mules by hard riding, left five companions behind —and still broke the **Trail** travel record by ten and a half days! This was the first of three unbelievable rides that Aubry made in 1848.

In mid March Aubry left Independence with his first train. He and 15 wagons arrived in Santa Fe in late April—before any other traders left Missouri. In May, Aubry planned a ten-day ride back to Independence to arrange another caravan.

By sending men ahead with extra horses, he was able to complete the trip in just eight days and ten hours! Along the way he left behind six companions, went three days without food, was captured and escaped from Comanches, slept only a few hours, rode three horses and two mules to death, and walked 40 miles to Fort Mann for a fresh mount.

The most amazing ride

Francis and his second wagon train arrived in Santa Fe in early August. Then, to prepare for his third caravan, he had to make another ride to Missouri. Again, he sent men ahead with fresh horses. He left Santa Fe at dawn on Tuesday, September 12. About 10 P.M. the following Sunday, he arrived in Independence—only five days and 16 hours later!

Alexander Majors met Aubry near **Rabbit Ears**. The rider only nodded "as the dust flew in our faces," the well-known freighter recalled. Aubry certainly did not have time to visit, for during that trip he claimed he slept only two and one-half hours, ate just six meals, rode 24 hours in the rain, was delayed by high water, traveled 600 miles in mud, ruined six horses, rode his favorite horse Dolly nearly 200 miles in 26 hours— and walked 20 miles!

With just a few hours rest, Aubry went on to St. Louis and bought more merchandise and wagons. He and his train left Independence in early October, traveling the **Mountain Route**.

The caravan finally arrived in New Mexico that winter, but not without problems. One man was killed by Indians, 150 mules were stolen or frozen to death, and most of Aubry's goods were ruined as the wagons plowed through snow 20 feet deep. Although he lost money on the caravan, Aubry proved three Santa Fe trips were possible in a year.

Twenty-seven Trail trips

In nine years, Aubry traveled the route of the Santa Fe Trail 27 times—including three round trips with wagons in both 1851 and 1852. By that time he had laid out his **Aubry Cutoff**, a Trail shortcut in western Kansas that avoided much of the dangerous **Jornada**. Fort Aubry (named after him, but often misspelled *Aubrey*) was later built near his cutoff. He also helped choose a railroad route from New Mexico to California. His travel journals were published nationwide.

Aubry, called "The Telegraph" and "Skimmer of the Plains," died in 1854. He was stabbed during an argument in a bar in Santa Fe. The adventurous young man was just 29.

***True Tales of Old-Time Kansas*, by David Dary (University Press of Kansas, 1984) *P*, tells of Aubry's record rides on the Trail. *François X. Aubry* by Donald Chaput (Arthur H. Clark Company, 1975) is the story of Aubry's life.**

Trail TRAVELER

Marion Russell

Women like Marion Sloan Russell proved that traveling the Santa Fe Trail wasn't for men only. At the age of seven, Marion made her first trip on the Trail—and she remained fascinated with its romance and adventure for the rest of her life.

Marion was born in Illinois in 1845. In 1852 Marion's mother Eliza decided to move her children from Kansas City to California. She planned to begin their journey on the Santa Fe Trail, but she did not have the $500 fare for herself, Marion, and her son Will. In return for passage, Eliza agreed to work as a cook on a U.S. Army supply train.

Traveling with the government wagons was one of Francis X. Aubry's **caravans**. Young Marion was proud to know the famous Aubry. "He was my friend, [with] young piercing eyes and boundless energy. In his heart was the lure of dim trails."

Children on the Trail

Marion described the Kansas prairies along the **Trail** as "a Persian rug, the lavender, red and yellow wild flowers mingling with the silvery green prairie grass. There were places where we saw wild turkeys among the cottonwood trees, and where the wild grapevines ran riot.... Sometimes we saw [buffalo] walking slowly in single file along their narrow paths on the way to a distant water hole."

One of Marion's jobs was gathering dried **buffalo chips** for the camp's cooking fires. "I would stand back and kick them, then reach down and gather them carefully, for under them lived big spiders and centipedes. Sometimes scorpions ran from beneath them. I would fill my long full dress skirt with the evening's fuel...."

Children on the Trail also had time for fun. Marion wrote of playing ball, leap-frog, and dare base in the evenings. In eastern Kansas, their playground was the "no-man's land" between the circles of camped wagons. But as the caravan moved into Indian country youngsters stayed inside the safety of the wagon circles.

Indians!

While camped at **Pawnee Rock**, Marion was "rudely awakened by the sound of Indian war whoops close at hand." Indians stampeded a large herd of horses that Aubry was taking to Fort Union. No one was killed, but they had to wait in camp several weeks while Aubry's men bought more stock in Leavenworth.

Eliza's money was stolen soon after they arrived in New Mexico, so she and the children stayed there instead of going on to California. Four years later, the family moved back east. Near Pawnee Rock, on that Trail trip, Will discovered the bodies of two trappers scalped by Indians. Eleven-year-old Marion watched wide-eyed as the victims were buried in a large homemade coffin.

They lived at Fort Leavenworth for a time, but Marion and Will were homesick for New Mexico. In 1860, the children were pleased when their mother decided to return west. On that trip they followed the **Mountain Route**. At **Bent's New Fort** Marion watched traders. "A white man would hold up something to trade. The Indians would crowd around [until one] would step forward and offer a blanket or a buffalo robe."

A Trail bride

In 1865 Marion married U.S. Army Lieutenant Richard Russell. Their wedding took place on the Trail, in the chapel at Fort Union. That summer, her husband was sent to Camp Nichols on the **Cimarron Route**. After begging his commander, Colonel "Kit" Carson, Marion was allowed to join Richard there. They lived in a tent, and later a **dugout**.

While Richard was on an escort mission to Fort Larned, she spent many lonely hours looking toward the Trail, "which lay like a discarded ribbon flung eastward by a giant hand."

"One evening," Marion wrote, "I saw a wagon train coming, hundreds of wagons escorted by a detachment of soldiers. There were wagons drawn by mules, oxen, and horses. There was a great herd of cattle. Soldiers rode in dusty ranks on either side of the caravan. Trembling, I arose.... A dusty lieutenant swept me a grand gesture. Lieutenant R.D. Russell had returned to his waiting bride!"

The Russells later lived near Trinidad, Colorado. In 1888 Richard was murdered during what was known as the Maxwell Land Grant War. Marion remained near Trinidad, where she died in 1936 at the age of 92. Sadly, after living through dangerous times on the Santa Fe Trail, she was struck and killed by an automobile—not far from the old Trail.

Learn more about Marion from her book, *Land of Enchantment* (University of New Mexico Press, 1981) P. Readers will notice her name is spelled *Marian* in the book, but that is a printing mistake. She always spelled her name *Marion*.

The Santa Fe Trail, 1610–1848

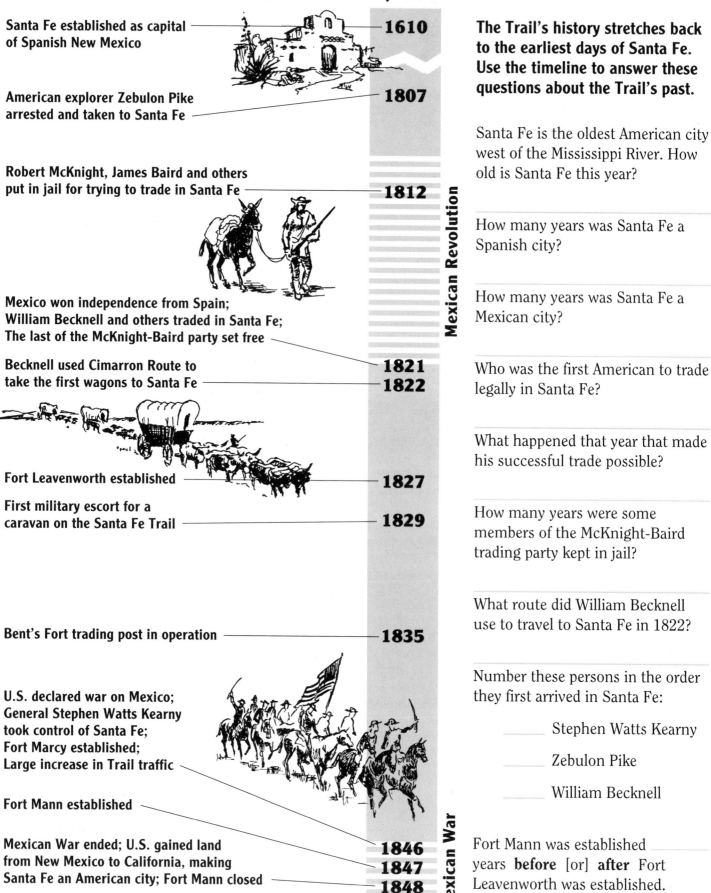

Santa Fe established as capital of Spanish New Mexico — 1610

American explorer Zebulon Pike arrested and taken to Santa Fe — 1807

Robert McKnight, James Baird and others put in jail for trying to trade in Santa Fe — 1812

Mexico won independence from Spain; William Becknell and others traded in Santa Fe; The last of the McKnight-Baird party set free — 1821

Becknell used Cimarron Route to take the first wagons to Santa Fe — 1822

Fort Leavenworth established — 1827

First military escort for a caravan on the Santa Fe Trail — 1829

Bent's Fort trading post in operation — 1835

U.S. declared war on Mexico; General Stephen Watts Kearny took control of Santa Fe; Fort Marcy established; Large increase in Trail traffic — 1846

Fort Mann established — 1847

Mexican War ended; U.S. gained land from New Mexico to California, making Santa Fe an American city; Fort Mann closed — 1848

Mexican Revolution / *Mexican War*

The Trail's history stretches back to the earliest days of Santa Fe. Use the timeline to answer these questions about the Trail's past.

Santa Fe is the oldest American city west of the Mississippi River. How old is Santa Fe this year?

How many years was Santa Fe a Spanish city?

How many years was Santa Fe a Mexican city?

Who was the first American to trade legally in Santa Fe?

What happened that year that made his successful trade possible?

How many years were some members of the McKnight-Baird trading party kept in jail?

What route did William Becknell use to travel to Santa Fe in 1822?

Number these persons in the order they first arrived in Santa Fe:

_____ Stephen Watts Kearny

_____ Zebulon Pike

_____ William Becknell

Fort Mann was established _____ years **before** [or] **after** Fort Leavenworth was established.

The Santa Fe Trail, 1849–1987

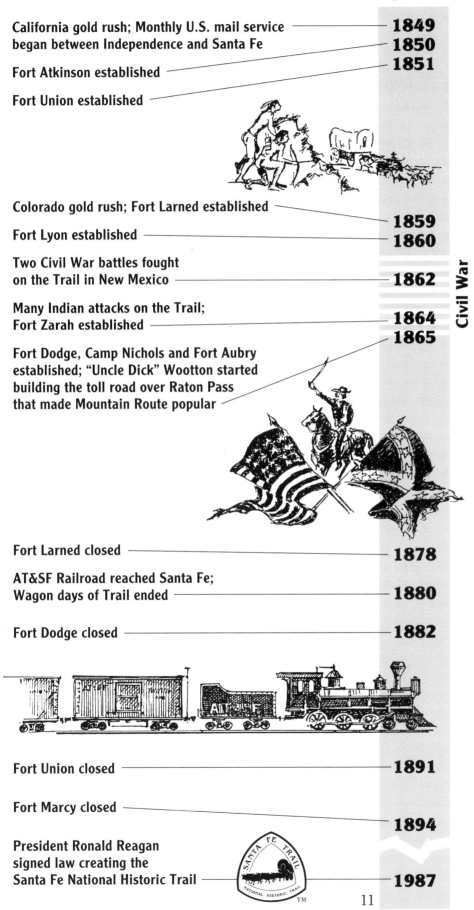

California gold rush; Monthly U.S. mail service began between Independence and Santa Fe — **1849**
— **1850**
Fort Atkinson established — **1851**
Fort Union established

Colorado gold rush; Fort Larned established — **1859**
Fort Lyon established — **1860**
Two Civil War battles fought on the Trail in New Mexico — **1862**
Many Indian attacks on the Trail; Fort Zarah established — **1864**
— **1865**
Fort Dodge, Camp Nichols and Fort Aubry established; "Uncle Dick" Wootton started building the toll road over Raton Pass that made Mountain Route popular

Civil War

Fort Larned closed — **1878**
AT&SF Railroad reached Santa Fe; Wagon days of Trail ended — **1880**
Fort Dodge closed — **1882**

Fort Union closed — **1891**
Fort Marcy closed — **1894**
President Ronald Reagan signed law creating the Santa Fe National Historic Trail — **1987**

Through the 1860s, the Santa Fe Trail was a busy road. Use the timeline to answer these questions about the history of the Trail.

Number these Trail forts in the order they were established:

_____ Fort Lyon

_____ Fort Aubry

_____ Fort Union

_____ Fort Larned

_____ Fort Zarah

Fort Larned closed _____ years **before** [or] **after** Fort Union closed.

Circle the fort that was open the greatest number of years:
Fort Dodge [or] **Fort Larned**

Fort Union was open _____ years.

Where did people "rush" to in 1859?

In what year were two Civil War battles fought on the Trail?

Who built a road over Raton Pass?

What happened 14 years after the AT&SF Railroad reached Santa Fe?

How many years has the Santa Fe Trail been a national historic trail?

Flags over the Trail

Santa Fe, Spain . . . Mexico . . . USA. Land along the Santa Fe Trail has changed hands over the years. These modern flags represent nine countries and states that have owned or claimed territory along the Trail since 1820. Identify each flag. (Names are missing from two of the flags.)

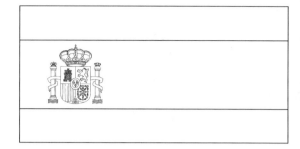

Flag of _____

Flag of _____

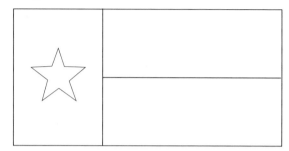

Flag of _____

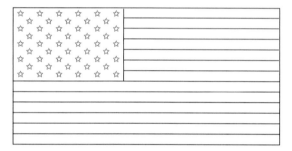

Flag of _____

Flag of _____

Flag of _____

Flag of _____

Flag of _____

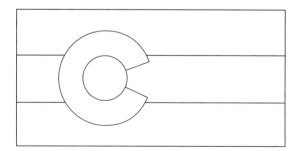

Flag of _____

What flags have flown over the place where you live?

¿Habla usted español?

Do you speak Spanish? Even if you don't, you probably understand several Spanish words. That's because many words in Spanish and English come from the same Latin roots. And, over the years, cultural links like the Santa Fe Trail have helped blend the two languages. Use Spanish words from this list to complete the paragraph below.

				metal	rápido
				mucho	rodeo
				nacional	señor
				olé	señora
				padre	señorita
				papá	sierra
				patio	siesta
				peón	sofá
actor	café	dentista	hotel	península	solo
adiós	capital	director	humor	peso	sombrero
adobe	central	doctor	idea	piano	sopapilla
amigo	cereal	error	lobo	piñata	tamale
ángel	chihuahua	explosión	loco	plan	taxi
animal	chili	favor	macho	plaza	televisión
bandido	chocolate	fiesta	magnífico	poco	toro
bonanza	club	frijoles	mamá	poncho	tortilla
bronco	color	gracias	mañana	pronto	unión
bueno	compadre	hacienda	matemáticas	pueblo	vaquero
burrito	corral	hombre	material	radio	violín
burro	coyote	hospital	mesa	rancho	vista

Recently my family visited Santa Fe. At the [town square] _____, we saw a monument that marked the end of the Trail. At a nearby [restaurant] _____ I ordered a [meat and peppers rolled in cornmeal and cooked in a cornhusk] _____. ["Thank you"] "_____" I told the waiter as he served me. That night, we were invited to a [celebration] _____. All the children were asked to help break a [clay or paper-maché figure stuffed with candy and toys] _____. When all the treats showered down, I was so excited my [mom] _____ said I was acting [wild or crazy] _____. The next day we went to Taos and toured an Indian [dwelling made of adobe or stone, often in levels] _____. My [dad] _____ bought a [wide-brimmed hat] _____ as a souvenir. He yelled ["hurray"] "_____" as he pretended to be a bullfighter fighting a [bull] _____. When our trip was over I hated to say [goodby] _____ to New Mexico.

What other Spanish words in the list do you know?

Routes to Santa Fe

On his 1822 trip William Becknell left from Franklin, Missouri. It was a popular **trailhead**, or starting point, for Santa Fe traders—until a flood on the Missouri River washed the town away in 1828. Other jumping-off points in the 1820s were Arrow Rock, Blue Mills, and Fort Osage, a small military **post** and trading center on the Missouri River.

Starting in the 1830s, many traders left from Independence. By about 1840, traders outfitted their wagons at Westport (now part of Kansas City, Missouri).

Marked by ruts

In the early years of the Santa Fe trade, parts of the **Trail** were not well marked. Streams, rivers, hills, mountains, large rocks, and other landmarks helped guide traders.

In 1825 the U.S. government sent surveyors to mark a Santa Fe road, beginning at Fort Osage. They built a few sod markers that soon disappeared in the weather, leaving traders to follow their own routes. (Apparently the surveyors' written report wasn't followed, either. It wasn't published for 125 years!)

Much of the Santa Fe Trail was eventually marked by the ruts left by passing wagons. In wet weather the heavy loads plowed deep tracks into the muddy sod. Even in dry times, thousands of wagon wheels and animal hoofs left wide, dusty paths on the prairie. In many places these ruts can still be seen today—after more than a century.

Campsites close to water

The list of Santa Fe Trail campsites is long. The places traders camped depended on the mileage their wagons traveled each day, as well as weather and the availability of water.

Many stopped at Round Grove, about 35 miles from Independence. Just west of there, the Santa Fe and Oregon Trails divided (after the Oregon Trail came into use in the early 1840s). At the Narrows, traders camped on a narrow ridge between Wakarusa Creek and the Marais des Cygnes river. Another popular spot was 110-Mile Creek. This creek was actually 95 miles from Independence, but the 1825 surveyors found it was 110 miles from Fort Osage.

Most wagons reached the Neosho River crossing at Council Grove after about ten days on the Trail. This first leg of the trip was a "shakedown" for freighters, teams, and equipment.

At Council Grove a blacksmith shoed animals and made wagon repairs. Freighters bought supplies at the "Last Chance" store. There were oak, walnut, and other hardwood trees nearby and most traders cut some timber to carry along for wagon repairs.

Most importantly, Council Grove was where **caravans** were organized. Farther west, the Trail was often dangerous, so independent traders grouped their wagons together for safety. The traders in a caravan elected a captain, other officers, and agreed on military-style rules.

Water was very important to caravans, of course, as shown by the names of other popular campsites in eastern Kansas: Diamond Spring, Lost Spring, Cottonwood Creek, Turkey Creek, the Little Arkansas

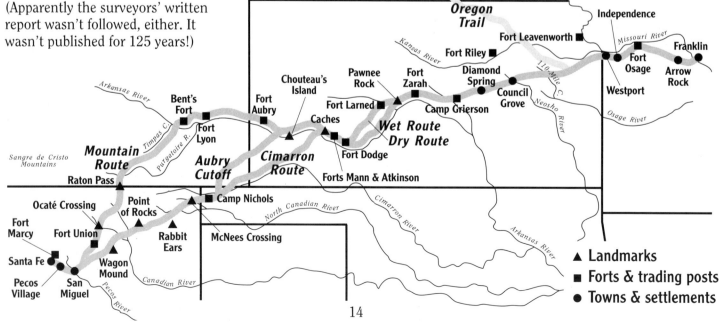

▲ Landmarks
■ Forts & trading posts
● Towns & settlements

Wagon Mound

River, Cow Creek, and the Big Bend of the Arkansas River. After reaching the Arkansas' Big Bend, the Trail followed the north bank of the river. Wagons passed Walnut Creek, **Pawnee Rock**, Ash Creek, the Pawnee Fork, and Coon Creek.

Near Pawnee Rock, the Trail divided for a distance. The **Wet Route** stayed near the Arkansas River, while the **Dry Route** took another course southwest. The Dry Route was easier to travel because the road was less sandy, but it often had no water. The two sections rejoined near where Fort Dodge was later located.

Dangerous country

As they headed west, caravans moved out of the tallgrass prairie onto the buffalo grass-covered plains. There they often met buffalo herds. This meant there was fresh meat to eat—and Plains Indians to deal with. However, the danger of Indian raids was not the only problem traders faced in that area. The lack of water was a worry as well.

When William Becknell went to Santa Fe in 1821, he was near sources of water much of the way. He followed the Arkansas River west into present Colorado, and then traveled south over the mountains into New Mexico. With his pack mules he was able to go over rocky trails through the Sangre de Cristo Mountains. On his second trip a year later, however, Becknell took three wagons. Because he knew his heavy equipment could not make it over the mountains, he crossed the Arkansas and headed for the Cimarron River.

However, between the two rivers Becknell's new route went about 60 miles without any reliable water sources. (Mexican traders called it the **Jornada**.) In 1823 one party ran out of water during their trip across this "Cimarron Desert." The traders were so thirsty they killed buffaloes and drank the blood! Even so, traders used the dangerous route for years. It was so dry that wagons left few marks on the hard soil. Some traders lost their way until that part of the Trail was marked by ruts in the wet year of 1834.

This **Cimarron Route**, or **Cimarron Cutoff** as it is sometimes called, followed the Cimarron River for about 70 miles, passing Middle Spring and Willow Bar. It then headed for Upper Spring and Cold Spring. (In 1851 trader Francis X. Aubry opened another route. His **Aubry Cutoff** left the Arkansas west of **Chouteau's Island** and joined the Cimarron near Cold Spring.) Travelers then passed McNees Crossing, **Rabbit Ears**, Round Mound, **Point of Rocks**, the Canadian River, and **Wagon Mound**.

Another choice

According to the trader Josiah Gregg, it was about 770 miles from Independence to Santa Fe over the Cimarron Route. Another choice was the way Becknell traveled in 1821—later known as the **Mountain Route**, **Mountain Branch**, Bent's Fort Route, or Raton Route. Some wagons began going that direction during the Mexican War, when the U.S. Army widened the narrow road through Raton Pass. The route became more popular after the Civil War. At that time Richens Lacy "Uncle Dick" Wootton built a **toll road** and collected money from travelers who used his road through the pass.

Some traders chose the Mountain Route because it offered more water and less danger from Indian raids. However, it was about 825 miles long and the extra 55 miles—part of it through mountainous **terrain**—meant several more days of travel for caravans anxious to reach Santa Fe.

Traders taking this route followed the north bank of the Arkansas to Big Timbers and on to **Bent's Fort**, an important trading post in present eastern Colorado. West of the post, the Trail left the Arkansas and headed southwest. It followed Timpas Creek, crossed the Purgatoire River, and topped Raton Pass.

The Trail then ran along the eastern edge of the Sangre de Cristo Mountains to Cimarron. From there some traders went west to Taos and then to Santa Fe. Most, however, headed south to Ocaté Crossing.

End of the Trail

Near Watrous, the Mountain Route rejoined the Cimarron Route. On the last section of the Trail, traders passed the settlements of Las Vegas, San Miguel, Pecos Village, and then went through Glorieta Pass in the Sangre de Cristos to Santa Fe.

Over the years—and as railroads built closer to New Mexico—new branches of the Trail were created. Other important routes used by Santa Fe traders were roads between Fort Leavenworth and the Trail; Fort Hays and Fort Dodge; Kit Carson, Colorado, and Fort Lyon; and Granada, Colorado, and Fort Union.

Trail TRAVELER

"Kit" Carson

"Kit" Carson is remembered as a legendary mountain man, scout, soldier, and Indian agent. On his first trip to the West, Carson was a runaway on the Santa Fe Trail.

Christopher Carson was born in 1809 in Kentucky, but his family moved to Missouri a few years later. After his father died, young "Kit" was apprenticed to a saddle maker in Franklin. Although Carson liked the man, he didn't want to spend the rest of his life making saddles. In 1826 he ran away.

Teenaged Kit wanted to see "different countries," so he joined a **caravan** headed to Santa Fe. Working as a herder, the young **greenhorn** soon saw the dangers of **Trail** life.

One of the men in their party accidentally shot himself in the arm. Infection set in, and it was obvious the limb would have to be amputated. Young Kit watched while a volunteer cut off the man's arm with a razor and saw. To stop the bleeding, the "doctor" heated a large wagon bolt in the campfire, burned the wound, and then covered it with tar from a wagon wheel! Amazingly, the injured man quickly recovered.

Mountain man and scout

Carson stayed in Santa Fe only a short time before moving on to Taos, the headquarters for mountain men. He spent the next several years trapping in territory from the Rocky Mountains, to California, and into the Black Hills. His companions included the famous mountain men Bill Williams and Jim Bridger.

In the early 1840s Kit traveled east with one of Charles and William Bent's caravans. After living in the wilderness for years, however, he was in St. Louis only a few days before he became uncomfortable.

To escape the "settlements," Kit climbed on a riverboat headed up the Missouri River. On board, he met the explorer John C. Frémont, who was preparing to make an expedition to the far West. Frémont offered Carson $100 a month to be his guide. Although Carson led the explorer through the Rockies to California and Oregon, it was Frémont who was later called "Pathfinder."

Back on the Trail

In 1843, Kit worked as a hunter for the Bent brothers' caravan. On one trip he rescued a group of Mexican traders when he rode alone through dangerous Indian territory to get them a military escort.

During the Mexican War, Carson guided General Stephen Watts Kearny and his troops from Santa Fe to California. From there, he carried messages back to the War Department in Washington, D.C.

On his way back to California, he was given an escort of 50 soldiers at Fort Leavenworth, for there were reports of Comanches along the Trail. As Carson and his men camped near **Pawnee Rock**, Indians attacked a nearby caravan of wagons and troops headed for the Mexican War. Kit helped chase the Indians away and recaptured most of the horses and oxen they had stolen.

After the Mexican War, Carson returned to New Mexico and began ranching at Rayado. But, while traveling the Trail in 1851, an Indian nearly ended Kit's life. Near **Chouteau's Island** he met a Cheyenne chief, upset about a whipping he had just received from an Army officer. The angry Indian was determined to kill the next white man he met—and that was Kit!

Carson managed to bluff his way out of danger by pointing out tracks on the Trail made by a passing squad of troops. He convinced the chief the soldiers would return quickly to rescue him—even though they were several days away on the Trail.

Trail commander

In 1852 Kit became Indian agent for the Jicarilla Apaches, Utes, and other tribes in the region. Then, at the start of the Civil War, he was made a colonel in the New Mexico Volunteer Infantry. During the next six years, he fought Confederates at the Battle of Valverde in New Mexico, Mescalero Apaches and Navajos in New Mexico and Arizona, and Kiowas and Comanches at Adobe Walls, Texas. He established Camp Nichols on the **Cimarron Route** in 1865 and then commanded Fort Union for a time.

Carson left the Army in 1867 and joined his family near Boggsville, Colorado. In the spring of 1868, his wife died at their ranch, after giving birth to their seventh child. Kit died a month later at nearby Fort Lyon. He was buried in Taos.

Three of the many books about Carson are *Kit Carson, Trail Blazer and Scout,** by Shannon Garst (J. Messner, Inc., 1942); *Kit Carson's Autobiography*, edited by Milo Milton Quaife (University of Nebraska Press reprint, 1966) P; and *'Dear Old Kit,' The Historical Christopher Carson*, by Harvey L. Carter (University of Oklahoma Press, 1968) P.

Trail TRAVELERS

"Buffalo Bill" and "Lissie" Mathewson

While others journeyed up and down the Santa Fe Trail, William Mathewson and his wife Elizabeth actually lived on it. At their road ranch they met traders, soldiers, Indians, and other Trail travelers.

William Mathewson was born in New York in 1830 and headed west at age 18. It isn't known when he first traveled the Santa Fe Trail, but by 1852 he was hunting in Colorado and New Mexico with "Kit" Carson. For the next few years Bill traded with Indians and trapped in the Rocky Mountains and across the Plains. Part of that time he worked for Bent, St. Vrain & Company.

'Dangerous Buffalo Bill'

In 1858 he helped Asahel and Abijah Beach build a trading post on the **Trail** at the Cow Creek crossing. It was there that Mathewson became "Buffalo Bill." (This was several years before the scout William F. Cody first used the famous nickname.)

In 1860 hundreds of farm families in eastern Kansas lost their crops to drought. When hungry settlers headed west to hunt buffaloes, Mathewson led them to the herds. He also did most of the killing—perhaps 80 buffaloes a day. Soon he was known as Buffalo Killer, and then, Buffalo Bill.

In 1861 Mathewson earned another nickname when he met the colorful Kiowa leader Satanta. The chief was angry that Bill had stopped some warriors from stealing horses, and he threatened to kill the trader. When Mathewson faced up to Satanta and beat him in a fistfight, Indians called him "Long-bearded, Dangerous Man." Satanta later brought Dangerous Man a gift of twenty ponies. The trader accepted the peace offering. He then returned the animals as a sign of friendship.

In 1862 Mathewson moved west on the Trail. He built a **road ranch**, or trading post, east of modern Great Bend. After a year he sold that store and joined trader Charles Rath at the nearby Walnut Creek crossing.

Trouble on the Trail

Mathewson returned to his Cow Creek ranch in 1864, a year of many **depredations** on the Santa Fe Trail. For three days that July, Mathewson and a handful of men defended their ranch against perhaps 500 Kiowas, Arapahoes and Comanches. (A legend says Satanta warned Bill of the attack.)

When the siege ended, Mathewson discovered that a nearby wagon train was also under attack. In a daring dash, he and his mare Bess charged through the Indian lines. Bill helped the frightened **teamsters** locate a shipment of rifles and ammunition in their train. The added firepower soon sent the Indians on their way.

A month later Bill married Elizabeth "Lissie" Inman. She was born in England in 1842 and had lived in St. Joseph, Missouri, since she was a girl. It is said that Mathewson didn't move his bride to Cow Creek until she became an expert with a rifle and revolver. With her husband, Lissie entertained famous Trail travelers, including newspaper correspondent Henry M. Stanley and U.S. Army generals William T. Sherman and Winfield Scott Hancock. She sold her homemade butter and cheese to travelers and managed the ranch when Bill was away. Other times, Lissie journeyed to St. Joseph or St. Louis to buy trade goods.

Peacemaker

In 1865 Mathewson helped arrange peace talks that led to the Treaty of the Little Arkansas. The next year Bill was appointed postmaster at Fort Zarah. He and Lissie apparently left Cow Creek at that time. (The water well is all that remains of their Santa Fe Trail ranch today.)

Mathewson again rode across the territory in 1867, helping gather tribes for a giant peace council near Medicine Lodge Creek. His reputation among the tribes also helped him arrange the release of white women and children held prisoner by Indians. Bill rarely talked about his adventures, but he may have helped free as many as 54 captives.

On a trip to Texas in 1867 to return two boys rescued from Comanches, Bill followed the Chisholm Trail. Part of the way on his return north, he guided one of the first herds of Texas cattle to travel that trail. That same year Lissie and a Missouri friend became the first white women to travel part of the Chisholm Trail. They went with Bill on a trading trip to Fort Sill in Indian Territory.

Wichita pioneers

The Mathewsons took a claim near Wichita in 1868. Bill and Lissie built one of the first houses in the future city, and for a time she was the only woman in town. She died there in 1885. Bill was a respected community leader. He established the Wichita Savings Bank and was the city police commissioner. The old plainsman died in Wichita in 1916.

Trail TRAVELER

William Bent

The Mountain Route of the Santa Fe Trail is sometimes called the Bent's Fort Route, named after the trading post built by William Bent and his brothers. "Kit" Carson once said of the famous Bents, "Their equals were never in the mountains."

William Bent was born in St. Louis in 1809. As a teenager, he went west in the 1820s with his older brother Charles, a fur trader. For two years William trapped and traded with Indians along the Missouri and Platte rivers. When Charles' fur company went out of business, the two brothers joined the Santa Fe trade to regain their lost money.

The Bents made their first Santa Fe trip in 1829—a dangerous year on the **Trail**. Charles led a **caravan** that Major Bennet Riley and 200 **infantry** soldiers escorted as far as the Mexican border (the Arkansas River in western Kansas).

Indians attacked them soon after they entered Mexican territory, but with help from Riley's troops—and later, some Mexican buffalo hunters and trappers from Taos—the Bents arrived safely in Santa Fe and sold their goods at a profit.

A daring idea

Charles continued in the Santa Fe trade, while William had other adventures. In Colorado, he had such good luck trading with Cheyennes and Arapahoes that he built a log stockade on the Arkansas River. Indians brought buffalo robes and beaver skins to exchange for powder, lead, knives, beads, and cooking pots.

By 1832, William had outgrown the small stockade, and he suggested a daring idea to Charles. Why not build a new trading post on the Arkansas? Using some of the $190,000 they had made as traders, the Bents and their partner Céran St. Vrain decided to build the largest trading post in the West.

Along with their younger brothers George and Robert, the two Bents hauled wagons of supplies from Santa Fe through the mountains—stubbornly chopping trees, moving boulders, and shoveling a path much of the way.

Bent's Fort

With advice from William's Cheyenne friends, they chose a site near the junction of the Arkansas and Timpas Creek, and during the summer of 1833, their fortress began to take shape.

Mexican workers made thousands of adobe bricks to build walls fourteen feet high around a group of rooms and a central courtyard. A heavy gate opened toward caravans arriving from the east. Tall towers at two corners gave a good view from all directions—and contained **loopholes** through which weapons could be fired. In back, a large adobe-walled corral could hold nearly 400 animals. To discourage raiders from climbing inside, the Bent brothers planted prickly cactus plants along the tops of the walls.

Bent, St. Vrain & Company named the **post** Fort William; everyone else called it **Bent's Fort**. Under William's management, the fort became the center of a huge fur trade network. Using goods and supplies shipped west from Missouri on the **Mountain Route** of the Trail, the company traded with Indians, Mexicans, and trappers—for furs, buffalo robes, blankets, sheep, horses, and mules.

During the 1840s three of the Bent brothers died. Robert was killed by Comanches, George died of a fever, and Charles (who had become the first American governor of New Mexico Territory), was murdered during a revolt in Taos. About the same time, William's Cheyenne wife died, after giving birth to a child.

Bent's New Fort

In 1849, the U.S. government wanted to buy Bent's Fort to use as a military post. William, upset by the recent deaths in his family—and perhaps angry at the government's low offer of $12,000—rolled kegs of gunpowder inside and destroyed much of his fort.

Four years later, William built a new stone trading post at Big Timbers, about 40 miles downstream on the Arkansas from his first fort. He did business at **Bent's New Fort** until he rented it to the government in 1860. (Because there were two Bent's Forts, historians now call his first one **Bent's Old Fort**.)

William then moved to a ranch at the mouth of the Purgatoire River. He stayed in the Santa Fe trade, and was an Indian agent for the Cheyennes and Arapahoes, respected by Indians and whites alike. Bent died at his Colorado home in 1869, after leading one last Trail caravan over Raton Pass.

David Lavender's book *Bent's Fort* (University of Nebraska Press reprint, 1972) P, tells William's story. Bent's Old Fort, near La Junta, Colorado, is a national historic site. It has been rebuilt by the National Park Service.

Mile after mile with Josiah Gregg

Josiah Gregg was one of the first traders to publish the mileage between places on the Santa Fe Trail. This table is adapted from his figures. Use it to answer the questions.

Miles from Independence		Miles between points
0	Independence	0
17	State Line	17
35	Round Grove	18
65	Narrows	30
95	110-Mile Creek	30
103	Bridge Creek	8
143	Big John Spring	40
145	Council Grove	2
160	Diamond Spring	15
175	Lost Spring	15
187	Cottonwood Creek	12
212	Turkey Creek	25
229	Little Arkansas River	17
249	Cow Creek	20
265	Arkansas River	16
273	Walnut Creek	8
288	Pawnee Rock	15
292	Ash Creek	4
298	Pawnee Fork	6
331	Coon Creek	33
367	Caches	36
387	Cimarron Crossing *(leave Arkansas River)*	20
437	Sand Creek	50
445	Cimarron River	8
481	Middle Spring	36
507	Willow Bar *(leave Cimarron River)*	26
525	Upper Spring	18
530	Cold Spring	5
555	McNees Creek	25
575	Rabbit Ear Creek	20
583	Round Mound	8
591	Rock Creek	8
610	Point of Rocks	19
630	Upper Canadian River	20
652	Wagon Mound	22
657	Santa Clara Spring	5
679	Río Mora	22
699	Las Vegas	20
716	Ojo de Bernal Spring	17
722	San Miguel	6
745	Pecos Village	23
770	Santa Fe	25

From what trailhead did Gregg measure his mileage?

Did his table follow the Cimarron Route or the Mountain Route?

Which state line did traders cross after 17 miles?

According to the table, how far was 110-Mile Creek from the beginning of the Trail?

If traders moved 15 miles a day, how many miles would they have gone after traveling six days?

At that same rate, what stream would they have reached after traveling 37 days from Independence?

If wagons had left Council Grove early on a Monday morning (still traveling 15 miles a day), on what evening would they have reached Lost Spring?

What point on Gregg's table was almost exactly halfway between Independence and Santa Fe?

How many Trail miles followed the Arkansas River?

Traders often found no water from the time they left the Arkansas River until they reached the Cimarron River. How many miles was that?

Find the mileage between Wagon Mound and Pawnee Rock:

Find the mileage between Cold Spring and Santa Fe:

How many days (at 15 miles per day) would traders have needed to travel from Cold Spring to Santa Fe?

Tracking the Trail across . . .

The Santa Fe Trail crossed parts of five states. Track the Trail on the maps (pages 21–24) by connecting these modern towns in order—New Franklin, Missouri to Santa Fe, New Mexico. To track the Mountain Route, connect the towns between Cimarron, Kansas, and Watrous, New Mexico. Parts of the Trail are already drawn.

Cimarron Route

MISSOURI	KANSAS (continued)	KANSAS (continued)
New Franklin	Admire	Montezuma
Franklin	Allen	Hickok
Petersburg	Bushong	Rolla
Arrow Rock	**Council Grove**	Wilburton
Hardeman	Wilsey	Elkhart
Marshall	Burdick	
Stanhope	**Lost Springs**	**OKLAHOMA**
Malta Bend	**Tampa**	Castaneda
Grand Pass	Durham	Wheeless
Waverly	Lehigh	**Mexhoma**
Dover	Canton	
Lexington	Galva	**NEW MEXICO**
Wellington	McPherson	Moses
Napoleon	Conway	Seneca
Levasy	Windom	Grenville
Sibley	Little River	Sofia
Independence	Mitchell	Farley
Raytown	Lyons	Abbott
Kansas City	Chase	**Colmor**
	Ellinwood	Levy
KANSAS	**Great Bend**	**Wagon Mound**
Leawood	**Pawnee Rock**	**Watrous**
Overland Park	**Larned**	Las Vegas
Lenexa	Garfield	**Romeroville**
Olathe	**Kinsley**	**Bernal**
Gardner	Offerle	**San Miguel**
Edgerton	Windhorst	**San Jose**
Baldwin City	Ford	**Rowe**
Overbrook	**Fort Dodge**	**Pecos**
Scranton	**Dodge City**	**Glorieta**
Burlingame	**Cimarron**	**Santa Fe**
Miller		

Mountain Route

KANSAS	COLORADO (continued)
Cimarron	Las Animas
Ingalls	**La Junta**
Charleston	Timpas
Pierceville	Delhi
Garden City	**Thatcher**
Holcomb	Tyrone
Deerfield	Model
Lakin	Hoehne
Kendall	**Trinidad**
Syracuse	**Starkville**
Coolidge	Morley
COLORADO	**NEW MEXICO**
Holly	**Raton**
Granada	**Colfax**
Lamar	**Cimarron**
Wiley	**Rayado**
McClave	**Ocate**
Hasty	**Watrous**
Fort Lyon	

Towns on the route of the Santa Fe Trail are in bold type.

Towns that are close to the Trail are in plain type.

This activity gives a general idea of the Trail's route. Gregory M. Franzwa's book, *Maps of the Santa Fe Trail* (The Patrice Press, 1989) *P*, is the best source for the exact route.

...northwestern Missouri...

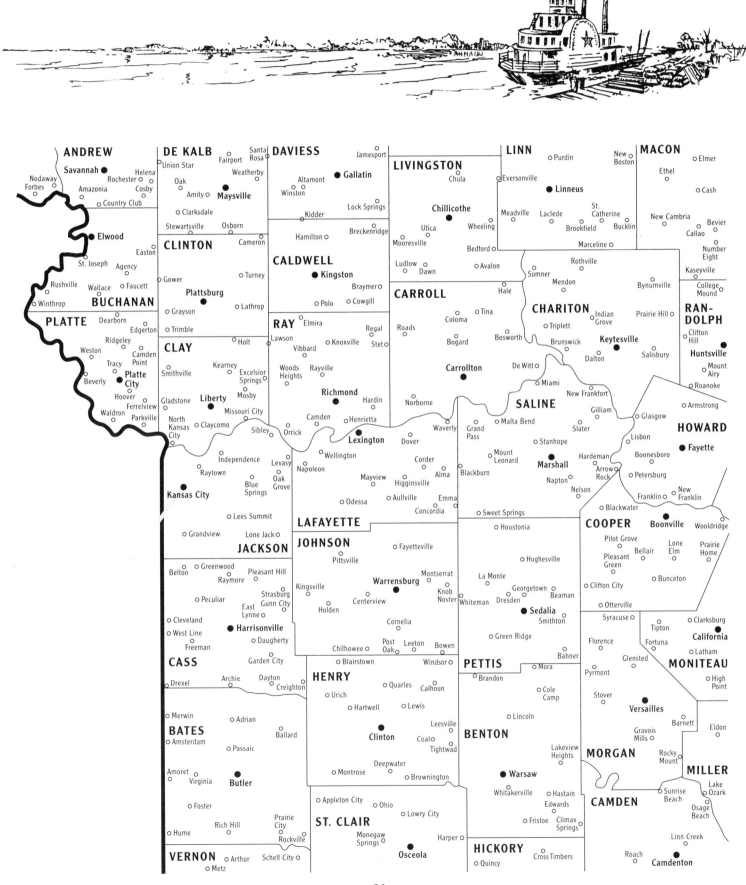

...western Kansas...

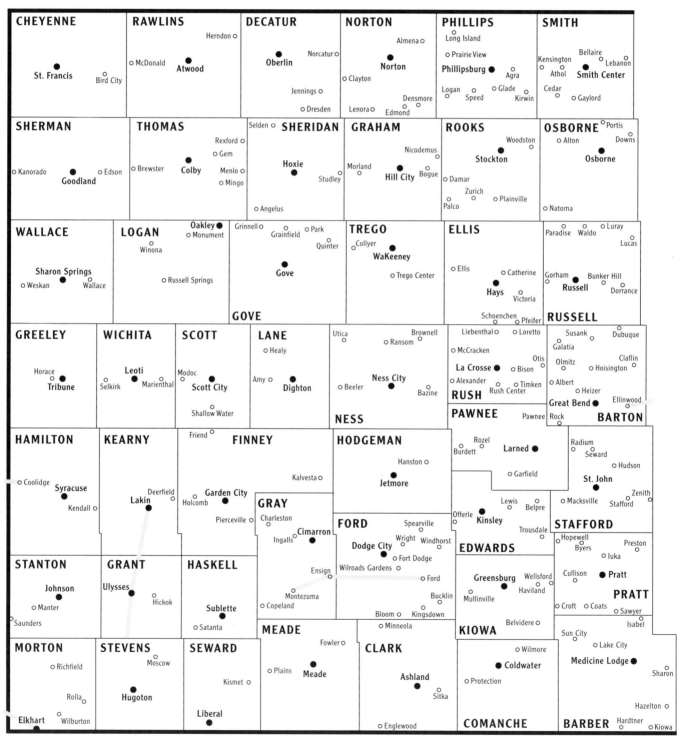

...eastern Kansas...

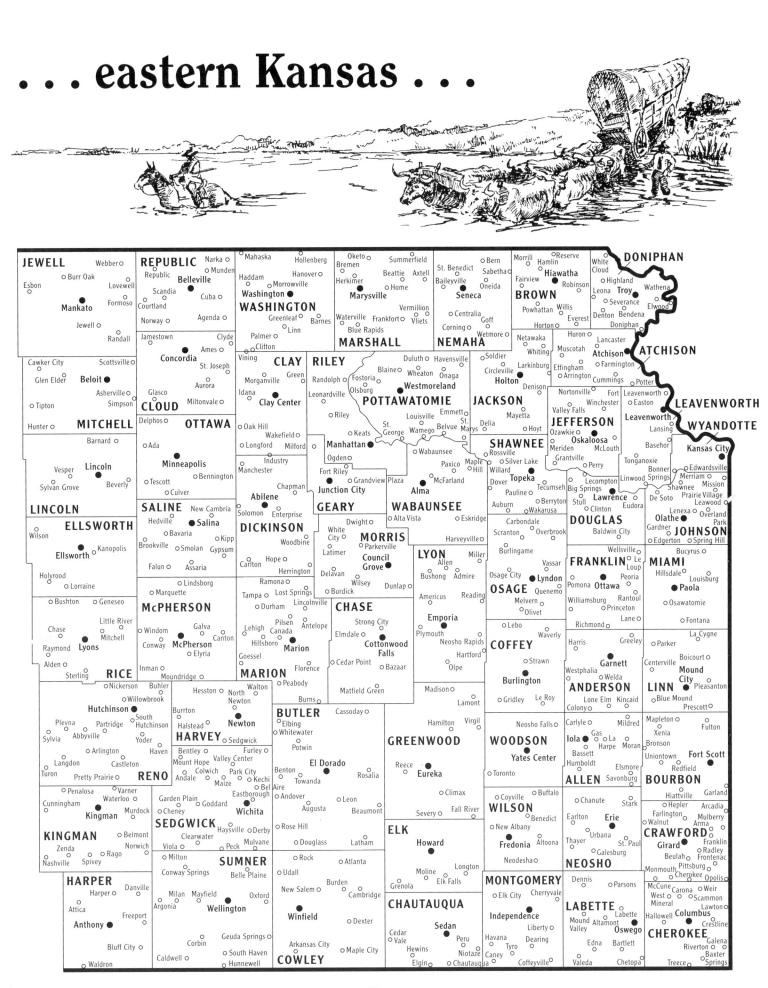

...and into New Mexico

Bent's Old Fort, Colorado

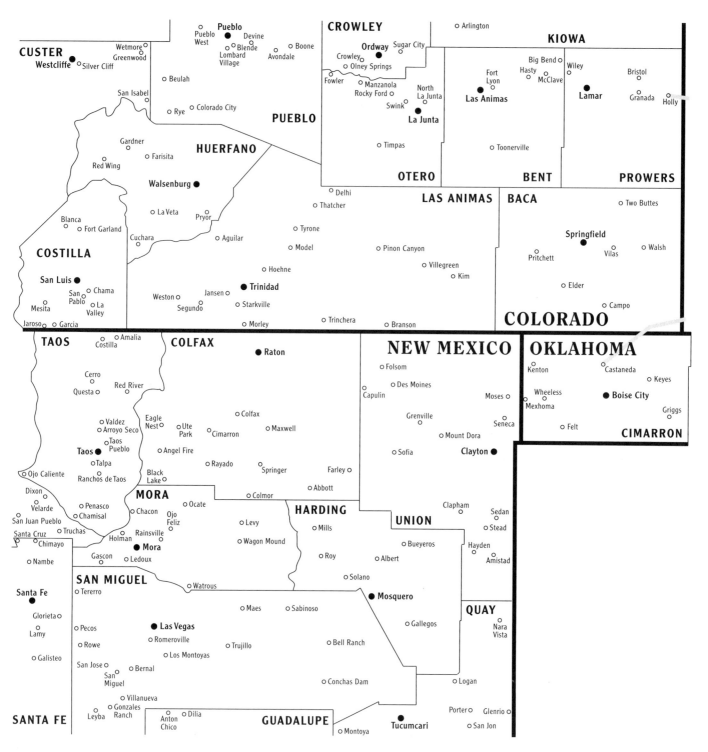

Mystery map

Chouteau's Island, Wagon Mound, and Rabbit Ears were all landmarks on the Santa Fe Trail. To identify them and other numbered mystery locations on this map, use the clues and the bold names below.

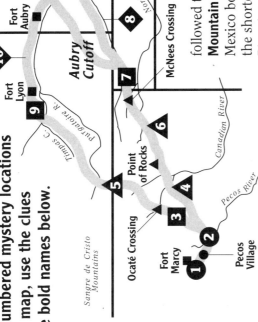

In early years, the Trail to **Santa Fe** began at **Franklin**, Missouri. In Kansas, **Council Grove**, at the Neosho River crossing, was an important campground. **San Miguel** was a small settlement on the Pecos River southeast of Santa Fe.

The eastern end of the Trail began on the **Missouri River**. Much of the Trail in western Kansas ran along the **Arkansas River**. Some traders followed the Arkansas on into Colorado—the **Mountain Route**. It crossed the Colorado-New Mexico border at **Raton Pass**. Other traders took the shorter **Cimarron Route** along the **Cimarron River** into the Oklahoma Panhandle.

Fort Osage was the most eastern fort on the Santa Fe Trail. Later, **Fort Leavenworth** was built north of the Trail along the Missouri River. **Fort Union** was located near the junction of the Mountain Route and Cimarron Route in New Mexico. **Fort Larned** was built near the eastern end of the Wet and Dry routes. **Fort Dodge** was located at the western end of those two routes.

Camp Nichols was the only military post on the Cimarron Route. **Bent's Fort** was a trading post (not a military fort) on the Mountain Route, between Timpas Creek and the Purgatoire River.

Pawnee Rock, the most famous Trail landmark in Kansas, was near the Big Bend of the Arkansas River. **Chouteau's Island** was farther west on the Arkansas. It was named after a French trapper who fought Pawnee Indians there before Trail days. **Wagon Mound** was east of Fort Union, New Mexico, and near the Canadian River. **Rabbit Ears** were two round-topped peaks southwest of McNees Crossing.

1. _____
2. _____
3. _____
4. _____
5. _____
6. _____
7. _____
8. _____
9. _____
10. _____
11. _____
12. _____
13. _____
14. _____
15. _____
16. _____
17. _____
18. _____
19. _____
20. _____
21. _____

Barrels, bundles, bales

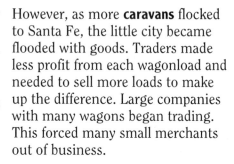

When William Becknell took the first wagons to Santa Fe in 1822, he packed merchandise that he felt sure would sell. The trader made wise choices, for he claimed he sold $3,000 worth of goods for $60,000. Because they were scarce in Santa Fe, he even sold a wagon valued at $150 for $700.

Cloth and hardware

Becknell's 1822 cargo probably included several kinds of cloth: muslin, drilling, print, taffeta, calico, broadcloth, linen, and velveteen. The Missouri trader also took other **dry goods**, clothing, buttons, buckles, handkerchiefs, razors, razor straps, writing paper, thread, needles, thimbles, knitting pins, scissors, pots, pans, coffee mills, knives, shovels, hoes, axes, and wine.

In the following years, most Santa Fe traders carried merchandise similar to Becknell's. Cloth, clothing, hardware, knives, sewing **notions**, jewelry, and religious objects were popular trade items in Santa Fe.

Before the Mexican War, the Mexican government had a list of **contraband** goods. Foreign traders were forbidden to sell (or were heavily taxed for) items such as iron, lead, gunpowder, candlewick, tobacco, and shoes. After New Mexico became American territory, freighters on the **Trail** hauled everything from military supplies and mining machinery to canned goods and bottled beer.

Money and mules

Missouri traders often returned home with gold and silver coins, silver **bullion**, gold dust, furs, blankets, wool, mules, and donkeys—cargoes that took little wagon room.

Since it was expensive to pull empty wagons, many traders sold or abandoned their extra equipment in Santa Fe. In the days of contraband, some traders burned wagons and sold the scrap iron illegally.

Profitable business

Traders' profits varied. When the Trail **commerce** was new and Mexicans were eager for American goods, many people made money.

A Missouri woman, Fanny Marshall, invested $60 in William Becknell's 1822 trip—and received $900 in return! Two years later, Meridith Marmaduke hauled $30,000 in goods to Santa Fe and returned east with gold, silver, furs, and mules worth $180,000.

However, as more **caravans** flocked to Santa Fe, the little city became flooded with goods. Traders made less profit from each wagonload and needed to sell more loads to make up the difference. Large companies with many wagons began trading. This forced many small merchants out of business.

At the same time, more and more wagons traveled to markets beyond Santa Fe. By 1840, one-half of all freight on the Trail went on south to Chihuahua and other cities. In the years just before the Mexican War, merchants from Mexico carried more Trail goods than Americans.

After the Mexican War large freighting companies contracted with American merchants and the U.S. Army to haul much of the Trail merchandise. The firm of Russell, Majors & Waddell made $300,000 from one large Army freighting contract in the 1850s.

Josiah Gregg estimated that in 1823 about $12,000 worth of goods was taken to New Mexico in just a few wagons. Twenty years later, the amount had grown to $450,000 worth of goods hauled in 230 wagons. By 1855, the trade was valued at about $5 million per year. At the end of the Civil War over 5,000 wagons a year were traveling the Trail.

What did shipping cost?

For many years, it cost about $8 to $10 to ship 100 pounds of merchandise on the Trail, or about a penny a pound per hundred miles. In fall and winter months, freighters charged higher rates because of the possibility of bad weather.

Shipping costs dropped as railroads built closer to New Mexico. In 1865, freighters hauled goods to Santa Fe from the railhead at Leavenworth for 14¢ a pound. Within six years, the cost was less than 2¢ a pound from Kit Carson, Colorado.

Trail TRAVELER

Antonio José Chávez

Antonio José Chávez was one of many Mexican traders who traveled the Santa Fe Trail. Sadly, he is remembered for his death—a murder on the Trail.

Chávez came from a wealthy and respected New Mexico family. Records of his birth have not been found, but it is believed Antonio José was born on the Chávez family estate at Los Padillas, perhaps about 1810.

Traders and politicians

Antonio José's family was active in the Santa Fe trade, as well as in New Mexico politics. His father was the first governor of New Mexico after Mexico won its independence from Spain in the 1820s. All of Antonio José's sisters married merchants in the Santa Fe trade.

Mariano, Antonio José's older brother, served as acting governor of New Mexico for a time. In 1846, a year after Mariano died, Susan Magoffin visited his widow. In her diary Susan described the Chávezes' large adobe home, with its "handsome" furnishings.

Mexican side of the trade

Antonio José and another older brother, José, married sisters who were the nieces of Manuel Armijo (governor of New Mexico before the Mexican War). Each of the Chávez brothers had his own home on the large family estate at Los Padillas. All three were involved in the Chávez family businesses—sheep ranching, gold mining, and the Santa Fe trade.

The Chávez brothers freighted merchandise from Missouri to Santa Fe, where it was sold or hauled on south to Chihuahua, Durango, and other Mexican markets. Each spring, they joined a **caravan** of New Mexico merchants who traveled east to buy American trade goods.

But Antonio José and his brothers were not the first New Mexican merchants in the Santa Fe trade. As early as the mid 1820s, New Mexicans used the **Trail**. Along with the American goods they sold in Santa Fe and other Mexican cities, the New Mexican merchants sold their own goods—mules, animal skins, sombreros, serapes, and other woven items.

By the 1830s, three-fourths of all the traders traveling south from Santa Fe toward Chihuahua were Mexican. In the 1840s, there were more New Mexican than American merchants on the busy **commerce** route between Missouri and Santa Fe. Captain Philip St. George Cooke, a U.S. Army officer, helped escort Trail caravans in 1843. He reported that one caravan of 140 wagons belonged entirely to Mexican owners.

Records show that José Chávez was on the Santa Fe Trail as early as 1839. It is possible young Antonio José made his first Trail trip (either as a passenger or a trader) with the 1840 caravan. But no one then knew that his last trip would come just three years later.

In 1843, trouble was brewing. Because Texas and Mexico were in the middle of a border conflict, a band of raiders from the Republic of Texas called "Texians" was plotting to rob caravans on the Trail. In Missouri, another group of Texas supporters was planning raids, too.

Murder on the Trail

Even though they knew of the danger, the Chávez family planned to send Antonio José east in February 1843. He was to buy merchandise in St. Louis. His brother José would then follow with the regular eastbound caravan in April.

Along the **Jornada** section of the **Cimarron Route**, Antonio José's small party ran into a fierce winter storm. Most of their mules died. Many of Chávez's frostbitten men deserted and returned to New Mexico. Antonio José and the rest of his party continued on, and he sent a servant ahead to bring help from Independence. Unfortunately, the servant was captured by the raiders from Missouri.

Near Cow Creek, the raiders met the rest of the New Mexicans and captured them, too. Antonio José and his men were held prisoner for several days while the Missourians divided the Chávez cash, gold, and furs. The thieves then turned the servants free. But, they killed Antonio José and dumped his body in a creekbed. Eventually, the raiders were captured and two of them were hanged for the Chávez murder.

'Chávez-Jarvis' Creek

The Kansas creek where Antonio José's body was left was later named for him. Over the years, however, *Chávez* Creek was mispronounced and misspelled until it eventually became *Jarvis* Creek.

Marc Simmons' book, *Murder on the Santa Fe Trail* (Texas Western Press, 1987) P, tells the story of Antonio José and his death.

Mariano Yrissarri's bill of goods

Mariano Yrissarri, a merchant in Albuquerque, often traveled the Santa Fe Trail to buy goods in Missouri. The list at right contains just a few of the items he bought in St. Louis in 1853. Use prices from the list to complete the invoice below. (In many cases, Mariano purchased goods priced by the dozen. Here, most prices are listed per item.)

Item	Unit price
Panama hats	$2.00 each
wool sombreros	1.25 each
straw sombreros	.88 each
girls' sombreros	.83 each
boys' caps	.71 each
flannel pants	2.00 per pair
damaged pants	.85 per pair
pantaloons	1.13 per pair
white shirts	.50 each
colored flannel shirts	.83 each
vests	.67 each
white stockings	2.25 per pair
colored stockings	1.25 per pair
white gloves	.75 per pair
mittens	1.50 per pair
wool shawls	1.50 each
coats	1.00 each
blue coats	.88 each
men's shoes	16.00 per pair
women's shoes	11.50 per pair
girls' shoes	2.75 per pair
boys' shoes	6.00 per pair
cotton yardage	.09 per yard
cashmere	.75 per yard
cambric linen	.14 per yard
canvas	.08 per yard
muslin	.22 per yard
black lace	.04 per yard
cotton umbrellas	.25 each
silk umbrellas	.88 each
feather dusters	.50 each
cups	.05 each
plates	.05 each
glasses	.05 each
forks	.13 each
spoons	.09 each
needles	.10 per hundred
fine-toothed combs	.07 each
mirrors	2.00 each
funnels	.05 each
lanterns	.33 each
tin pails	.19 each
assorted nails	5.25 per barrel
carriage whips	.21 each
violin strings	.50 per bundle
ink	.03 per bottle
writing paper	.67 per ream
wallpaper	.13 per piece

INVOICE

Quantity	Item	Unit price	Total price
6	boys' caps		
7	girls' sombreros		
6 pairs	men's shoes		
8	vests		
9	colored flannel shirts		
7 pairs	damaged pants		
3	coats		
9 pairs	mittens		
30 yards	cotton yardage		
11 yards	cambric linen		
12 yards	black lace		
250	needles		
5	mirrors		
15	funnels		
9 reams	writing paper		
5 bottles	ink		
		Invoice total	

Which of the items in the list are priced close to what you might pay today?

Josiah Gregg's graphs

Josiah Gregg made several trips to Santa Fe as a trader in the 1830s. The figures at right are from *Commerce of the Prairies*, a book he wrote in 1844 about the Santa Fe Trail. Use Gregg's table to complete the graphs showing Trail traffic over the years.

Year	Goods	Wagons	Men
1822	$15,000	3	70
1823	12,000	?	50
1824	35,000	26	100
1825	65,000	37	130
1826	90,000	60	100
1827	85,000	55	90
1828	150,000	100	200
1829	60,000	30	50
1830	120,000	70	140
1831	250,000	130	320
1832	140,000	70	150
1833	180,000	105	185
1834	150,000	80	160
1835	140,000	75	140
1836	130,000	70	135
1837	150,000	80	160
1838	90,000	50	100
1839	250,000	130	250
1840	50,000	30	60
1841	150,000	60	100
1842	160,000	70	120
1843	450,000	230	350

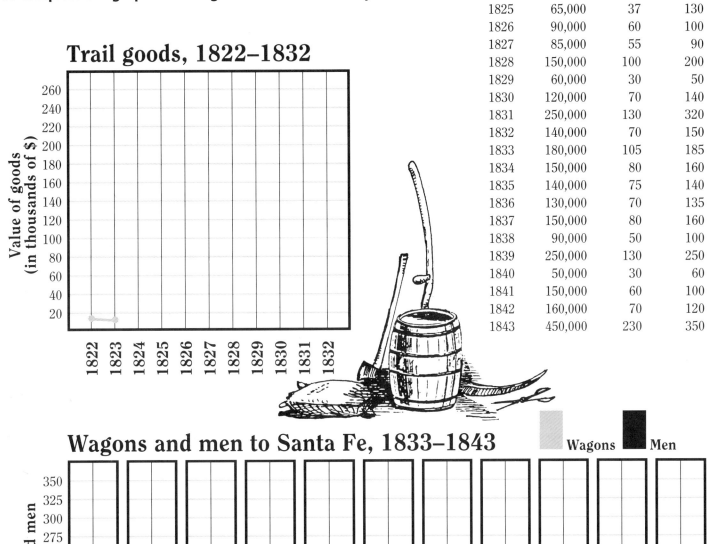

In most years, how did the number of men compare to the number of wagons?

J.J. Webb's puzzling list

James Josiah Webb, a trader, wrote about his Trail experiences in a book, *Adventures in the Santa Fé Trade* (Porcupine Press reprint, 1974). In it he listed items he took to New Mexico in the 1840s. Find 33 of them in the puzzle.

- hairpins
- hickory shirts
- buck gloves
- thread
- brass nails
- rings
- pins
- shawls
- straps
- blue denims
- coffee mills
- hooks
- needles
- spades
- cork inkstands
- black silk
- necklaces
- percussion caps
- white cotton hose
- pearl shirt buttons
- padlocks
- silk ties
- bonnet ribbons
- flannel
- shovels
- log chains
- coat buttons
- Irish linens
- French lawns
- tacks
- satin jeans
- butcher knives
- ivory combs
- razors
- candlewick
- suspenders
- axes
- beads
- drillings
- soap
- scissors
- pocket knives
- muslins
- iron spoons
- sadirons
- saw files
- prints
- vest buttons
- handkerchiefs
- calicoes
- pongee
- cambric
- alpaca
- sheeting
- hoes
- cashmere

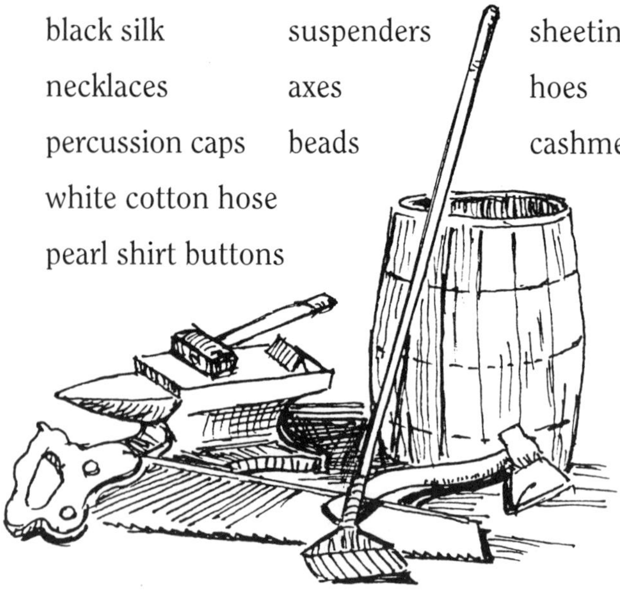

Which cloth does not come from a plant?
  French lawns [or] **cambrics** [or] **alpaca**

Who would use a percussion cap?
  a musician [or] **a soldier** [or] **a costumer**

Who would use drillings?
  a dentist [or] **a seamstress** [or] **a miner**

Cashmere is made from _____.

A sadiron is used to _____.

Coffee mills are used to _____.

```
P A O S P A R T S L E
I C S A B G A P K A M
C A N D L E W I C K S
L L E I U P R N O B P
E I N R E N A S L L A
A C I O D E Z C D A C
S O L N E E O D A C N
R E H S N D R S P K O
E S S T I L S K O S I
D R I N M E T C D I S
N B R A S S N A I L S
E L I E E R E T E K U
P A O D I B A V A T C
S H A W L S O Y X I R
U P E N T H I B E E E
S C I S S O R S S S P
T H R E A D E W K L H
N O I C I R B M A C O
I R O N S P O O N S O
R L O G C H A I N S K
P O N G E E R I N G S
```

J.J. Webb's trade items

James Josiah Webb was a Santa Fe trader for over 15 years. Below are some of the items he took down the Trail in the 1840s. Group them into categories. Use a dictionary to help sort unusual items.

cotton thread	necklaces	drillings
brass nails	padlocks	vest buttons
gold rings	silk ties	knives
pins	soap	muslins
percussion caps	flannel	iron spoons
axes	shovels	sadirons
shawls	log chains	prints
hickory shirts	coat buttons	cambric
buck gloves	Irish linens	alpaca
razor straps	French lawns	hoes
blue denims	tacks	cashmere
hooks & eyes	satin jeans	handkerchiefs
needles	saw files	calicoes
spades	ivory combs	pongee
cork inkstands	candlewick	hairpins
black silk	suspenders	cotton hose
bonnet ribbons		
beads		

Dry goods

Sewing notions

Hardware

Jewelry

Miscellaneous

Hard work, long hours

Not counting passengers, wagon trains to Santa Fe usually carried one or two men for each wagon. An average-sized **caravan** had 26 wagons—25 full of cargo, and one carrying supplies. A train that size needed 32 to 36 men.

Men on the **Trail** came from many backgrounds—American, Mexican, African American, German, English, Irish, French, and Native American. During the eight-week trip, they worked hard over many long hours. Much of the time, they walked or rode in clouds of burning alkali dust. Buffalo gnats buzzed in their ears all day. At night mosquitoes often made sleeping impossible. Even so, many men were called "vigorous, rollicking, devil-may-care."

They carried a variety of weapons: rifles, shotguns, pistols, and knives. Their clothing was a frontier "grab-bag" of leather hunting shirts, red cloth shirts, flannel vests, blue jean jackets, and merchants' fancy coats. No matter what they wore, at the end of the Trail everything was covered with dust, mud, sweat, food grease, tobacco juice, and manure.

Trail bosses

In private trains, one **wagonmaster**, or trail boss, was in charge of the whole wagon train. He made the rules that everyone followed. Some wagonmasters, like Alexander Majors, said that their trains would not travel on Sundays. Majors also asked his men to sign pledges against whipping their animals, and using profane language or liquor.

The wagonmaster rode ahead of the caravan to choose the next campsite. He also watched for bad places in the road, picked spots to cross streams, and scouted for Indians. His salary was the highest of all the men working on a train, or about $150 a month (in the 1860s).

The assistant wagonmaster received about $85. He kept slower wagons moving and helped new **greenhorns** learn their jobs. The assistant rode at the end of the train.

'Whackers and 'skinners

There was one **teamster**, or driver, for each wagon; **bullwhackers** drove oxen and **mule skinners** drove mules. Teamsters were paid $70 to $75 a month, with mule skinners usually getting more than bullwhackers.

No bullwhacker was without a bullwhip—some up to 20 feet long. It took two hands to crack the buckskin "poppers" at the end of the longest whips, but some drivers could flick flies off an ox's ear without hitting the animal. A bullwhacker shouted commands to control his animals: "gee" to turn right, "haw" to turn left, and "whoa" to stop. A mule skinner rode the **nigh** mule on the team nearest the wagon. He controlled his animals with reins.

Other men were paid about a dollar a day. Two day herders and one night herder took care of the extra stock—30 to 40 mules or oxen to replace animals that wore out along the way. Three or four extra men were often hired to replace those who deserted or became ill or injured.

Divisions of men

Wagonmasters usually organized their men at Council Grove. Large caravans were formed into groups of 25 wagons. Each of these divisions chose a captain, lieutenant, and a sergeant of the guard. All men in the train (whether workers or travelers) were divided into groups of eight called **reliefs**. Each relief had to stand guard one-fourth of the night, every other night.

The men were also divided into cooking groups. Each **mess** had from eight to twelve members and its own cooking equipment. Usually, one man did the cooking. The others shared the jobs of getting water, gathering wood or **buffalo chips** for fuel, and cleaning up.

Bacon, beans, bread

Most freighters gave their men a daily food **ration**. For each man that he cooked for each day, a cook could use one and one-fourth pounds of flour, about a pound of **sowbelly**, one and one-fourth ounces of coffee, and two and one-half ounces of sugar. There were usually enough beans for one meal per week and enough dried apples for an apple dish twice a month. When caravans reached buffalo country, most cooks used fresh buffalo meat. But menus were still tiresome.

Many men were poor cooks and even good cooks had a hard time preparing food on the Trail. There was never enough sugar. The sowbelly was dried, salted—and "indestructible." Nothing made it better or worse, one man wrote. He went on to say that anything made from flour—bread, biscuits, or flapjacks—was "a scurvy, dispepsia-breeding, muddled mess."

Trail TRAVELER

Alexander Majors

Alexander Majors was familiar with the jobs on a wagon caravan, for he was a partner in one of the largest freighting companies on the Trail.

Majors was born in Kentucky in 1814. He became a freighter on the Santa Fe Trail in 1848 after he decided his three young daughters would not be able to help him run his Missouri farm.

A gentleman's pledge

As he hired **teamsters** for his first trip to Santa Fe, Majors did something that would make him well-known across the West.

He made each man sign a pledge: "While I am in the employ of A. Majors, I agree not to use profane language, not to get drunk, not to gamble, not to treat animals cruelly, and not to do anything else that is incompatible with the conduct of a gentleman. And I agree, if I violate any of the above conditions, to accept my discharge without any pay for my services."

Majors, a devout Christian, also gave each driver a Bible. He insisted that his train pause all day on Sundays for preaching and meditation. On that first trip, he made nearly $4,000. And his **caravan** traveled to Santa Fe and back in record time for an ox-powered train—92 days.

Some said that Majors' men (nicknamed "Bible-Backs") did not always follow his strict rules. However, those who joked about Majors and his ideas came to respect him as they saw his success on the **Trail**.

Within a few years, he owned 100 wagons and was the leading freighter in Missouri.

Still, Alexander continued to work alongside his employees. Sometimes he acted as a **wagonmaster**; other times he walked beside the teams. When he had more than one caravan on the Trail, he rode back and forth between them. At night he shared stories and prayers with his men around the campfire, and slept on the ground under a wagon.

On one trip he witnessed a prairie phenomenon—a mirage. Along the **Cimarron Route** some **cavalry** soldiers approached his train, but "the horses' legs looked to be from 15 to 18 feet long." He recalled: "The body of the horses and the riders upon them presented a remarkable picture, apparently extending into the air, rider and horse, 45 to 60 feet high. . . . At the same time I could see beautiful clear lakes of water. It was a marvel."

Practical Trail advice

Majors was a very practical man. He soon learned the best ways to handle caravans on the Trail. "Much depended upon the skill of the wagonmasters," he wrote. He hired leaders who could keep the men disciplined, yet working in "perfect harmony."

Oxen, he felt, were the "cheapest and most reliable teams for long trips." When they had plenty of grass and were well-treated, he found they could travel 2,000 miles in a season. He also noted that the animals in one caravan usually left enough **cow chips** at a campsite to furnish fuel for the next caravan.

Partnerships and problems

Majors began moving supplies for the government in 1854. The next year he and a new partner, William Russell, took over all of the U.S. Army's freighting west of the Missouri River. The partners hired 1,700 men and had them sign his pledge. One of them was a young wagon messenger, William F. Cody—later known as "Buffalo Bill."

Russell & Majors made over a quarter of a million dollars from their first contract, and soon owned nearly 400 wagons. In 1858 the Army offered a large two-year contract. Majors and his partner joined William Waddell and formed the firm of Russell, Majors & Waddell; the partnership quickly landed the huge government job.

To handle the freighting, their company used nearly 150 trains—with 4,700 wagons, 4,600 men, and over 50,000 oxen and mules. Wagonmasters were given instructions based on Majors' rules. Unfortunately, bad weather, Indian **depredations**, and other problems caused the firm to lose thousands of dollars.

For a time, Majors and his partners tried operating stagecoaches and the famous Pony Express, but those ventures failed too. Their partnership ended in 1862. Majors continued freighting for a few years and later worked for the Union Pacific Railroad. He died in Chicago in 1900.

Majors' Kansas City home is now a museum. He wrote a book about his freighting experiences called *Seventy Years on the Frontier* (University of Nebraska reprint, 1989) P. A.M. Anderson and Adolph Regli's book *Alec Majors: Trail Boss* * (Wheeler Publishing Company, 1953) also tells Majors' story.

Trail TRAVELER

Robert Wright

Robert Wright held several different Trail jobs—from a tenderfoot teamster to a successful merchant.

Wright was born in Maryland in 1840 and moved to the West at the age of 16. He made his first trip on the Santa Fe Trail as a young **bullwhacker** in 1859.

Phantom Indians

At **Pawnee Rock**, the **greenhorn** had what seemed to be a close call. When the **caravan** camped beside the famous landmark, young Robert and another man were given the first watch of the night.

Several hours passed, and then suddenly: "We were startled by something dropping, *zip! zip!* into the grass around us and near us. We thought it was Indians shooting at us with arrows, . . . but the question was, where were they concealed?"

Wright and his friend woke the **wagonmaster**, who solved the mystery. The phantom "Indians" were skylarks, flitting their wings in the darkness, and landing with a noise that sounded like falling arrows.

Old Dan's stampede

By 1862 Wright was "bullwhacking" for Russell, Majors & Waddell. As he learned while camped near the Arkansas River that fall, it took very little to frighten oxen into stampeding.

One morning Robert was driving a tame steer named Old Dan back into camp. Because the weather was warm, Wright took off his coat and hung it over the old ox's horns—with the red and yellow lining flapping in Dan's face.

As they neared the caravan, the other animals were in their **yokes** and ready to roll. One young steer saw Old Dan's strange, colorful headdress and let out "a long, loud, beseeching bawl." Quickly, other animals bellowed and ran—causing what Wright called "one of the most disastrous stampedes in the history of the Plains."

When the dust cleared, six wagons lay smashed in Walnut Creek, with wreckage from a dozen more spread out over ten miles of the **Trail**. Three steers and a man had broken legs, and loose animals were scattered for 15 miles. During the cleanup, the wagonmaster rode up and asked Wright if he knew what had started the stampede. Probably a wolf, the young bullwhacker answered.

Dutchman in a dugout

A few years later, Robert worked for a Trail stage line that ran coaches between Kansas City and Santa Fe—over 700 miles in seven days. He built and operated the stage stations between Fort Dodge and Fort Lyon.

The stations, about 40 miles apart, were **dugouts** cut into the banks of the Arkansas River. To run his Pretty Encampment station west of old Fort Aubry on the **Mountain Route**, Wright hired a Dutchman named Fred. But he was afraid of Indians, and kept threatening to quit. "Fred was a big burly devil, strong as an ox, but a big coward," Wright wrote.

One morning as he was riding to Pretty Encampment to give his frightened employee a "pep talk," Wright met him running along the Trail. Fred was covered with blood and his clothes were torn. He was waving a big, sharp butcher knife and screaming, "I killed him! I cut his throat and his guts out!"

Wright led the Dutchman back to the station, expecting to find a dead Indian—and perhaps other angry tribesmen. Instead, he found a demolished dugout with bloody buffalo remains inside. In the night, an old bull had fallen through the sod roof. Poor Fred, thinking he was being attacked by Indians, had wrestled and killed the big animal in the dark!

Tragic times, too

Travel on the Santa Fe Trail often "had a much more tragic ending," as Wright pointed out. A few days after Fred's experience, two wagon drivers were killed in the same area.

More than once Wright found evidence of "mysterious bloodshed" along the Trail: ownerless mules and oxen, abandoned wagons and buggies, scattered trade goods, and even a beautiful horse with an empty blood-covered saddle. When Indians attacked Wright's ranch near the Trail, his wife and children escaped the **depredation** only by slipping away and floating down the Arkansas River in a canoe.

Later, Robert Wright was the **sutler** at Fort Dodge. He also helped establish Dodge City. There he was a respected businessman, politician, farmer, and rancher. He died in Dodge City in 1915. The Ford County community of Wright, northeast of Dodge City, was named for him.

Wright's autobiography, *Dodge City, The Cowboy Capital*, was first published in 1913. It was later reprinted (Arno Press, 1975), but both versions are out of print.

Trail work and wages

Most jobs on a Santa Fe Trail caravan are in the categories below. Complete this table with information from "Hard work, long hours" (page 32). Then use multiplication and addition skills to find the total monthly wages for everyone in an average-sized caravan. (An average-sized Trail caravan had 26 wagons.)

Trail job	Job nickname(s)	Important job responsibilities	Number in a caravan	Monthly wages (per man)	Monthly wages (for all)
Wagonmaster					
Assistant wagonmaster					
Teamsters					
Herders					
Extra hands	(none)				
				Total monthly wages	

Bosses, teamsters, herders

Work on the Santa Fe Trail was tiring and often dangerous, but the men who moved the heavy wagons were tough. Use facts from "Hard work, long hours" (page 32) to complete this outline of Trail jobs. The phrases below will help.

Answers

Two men in daytime, one at night	Herders
Replaced deserters or sick men	Teamsters
Three or four men per caravan	Drove mules
Earned about $150 a month	Bullwhackers
Earned about $75 a month	Wagonmaster
Chose campsites and route	Mule skinners
Kept slow wagons moving	Helped greenhorns
In charge and made rules	Scouted for Indians
Picked stream crossings	One man per wagon
Assistant wagonmaster	Rode near end of train
Carried a bullwhip	Rode ahead of caravan

I. Trail bosses
  A. _____
    1. One man per caravan
    2. _____
    3. _____
    4. _____
    5. _____
    6. _____
    7. _____
  B. _____
    1. One man per caravan
    2. Earned about $85 a month
    3. _____
    4. _____
    5. _____

II. _____
  A. _____
    1. One man per wagon
    2. Drove oxen
    3. Earned about $70 a month
    4. _____
  B. _____
    1. _____
    2. _____
    3. _____

III. Other men
  A. _____
    1. Earned about $30 a month
    2. _____
    3. Took care of extra stock
  B. Extra hands
    1. Earned about $30 a month
    2. _____
    3. _____

On the march

A day on the Santa Fe Trail began before dawn. If the cook fixed breakfast, he cried: "Bacon in the pan—Coffee in the pot—Get up and get it—While it's hot!" On other trains, the night herder woke the crew and they didn't eat until noon.

Hitch 'em up

First, the animals were hitched. With ten to twelve mules or oxen for each wagon, a 26-wagon **caravan** had 300 or more animals to be rounded up, sorted, and hitched. At first, it was a noisy, confusing, and time-consuming job. After several days on the **Trail**, however, many **wheelers**, **pointers**, **swingers**, and **leaders** learned to move quietly into their correct places each morning.

Alexander Majors once timed one of his crews, and found they could **yoke** six pairs of oxen and hitch them in 16 minutes. Another man claimed he could yoke and hitch his outfit in only five minutes.

About 15 miles a day

On the Trail, loaded ox-powered trains covered about 12 to 15 miles a day—or one and one-half to two miles per hour. At two and one-half miles an hour, loaded mule trains went farther—about 15 to 20 miles a day. Wagons returning from Santa Fe were lighter and moved faster.

Many things affected how fast caravans actually traveled: **terrain**, weather, weight of the cargo, experience of the **teamsters** and animals, water and grass, Indians, or other emergencies. Outfits with new men and untrained animals sometimes made only two miles the first day out. A wagon train crossing rugged Raton Pass in 1846 traveled just a few hundred yards one day. That same year, a U.S. Army caravan with heavily loaded wagons moved 45 miles a day for several days over more level country.

Caravans in columns

Large trains usually did not travel in one long line. Depending on the weather, it was often too dusty or muddy for the men and animals at the end of the line. Instead, many caravans traveled in two shorter columns. After they reached the Little Arkansas River, most westbound trains divided into four columns. In case of trouble the four "wings" could quickly group into a small four-sided fortress.

In some trains, the **bullwhackers** or **mule skinners** drew lots for their positions in the line of march. Other times, the best drivers led each column. The rest fell into line behind, with the newest drivers at the rear. During the trip, most **wagonmasters** rotated the order so no one had to "eat dust" all the way. (On days with little wind, huge dust clouds were stirred up by the wagon wheels and animal hoofs. At times, travelers reported seeing dust from a moving caravan 20 miles away.)

A long day

Once on the move, a caravan usually traveled until about ten A.M. Teams were unhitched and allowed to drink, graze, and rest while crews ate their biggest meal of the day. Afterward, men repaired wagons, yokes, harnesses, **singletrees**, or **doubletrees**. They also greased wagon wheels, doctored animals, hunted, and did other needed work. Most caravans then traveled from about two until six P.M. If the weather was very hot, some traders stayed longer in their noon camp and drove a few hours in the moonlight.

When caravans stopped overnight at a stream or river crossing, wagons always forded before making camp. If not, a rainstorm in the night could flood the stream and delay the train for several days. Also, **draft animals** were more willing to pull heavy wagons through streams in the evening than when they were stiff and sore in the morning.

In the overnight camp, crews took care of the animals before they ate. Later, if there were no repairs to do, men had time to relax. Some visited or told stories, others sang, smoked, or played cards.

Rest for the weary

Some freighters tried to let their animals and men rest one day a week. Alexander Majors insisted his caravans remain in camp each Sunday. Others rested two different half-days during the week, wherever good water and grass could be found.

Trail VOICES
Weather

James Ross Larken journeyed west with William Bent in the fall of 1856. The 25-year-old had health problems, and he made his Trail trip on Bent's caravan hoping to find a "prairie cure." Larken's diary has been published in *Reluctant Frontiersman*, edited by Barton H. Barbour (University of New Mexico Press, 1990) *P*. Along the Arkansas River his party traveled in rain:

"Oct 9th After travelling a good distance[,] camped near the Arkansas —there being a storm coming up— Had hardly got settled down before on it came, raining & blowing a gale—during the night the thunder & lightning was tremendous—I was quite uneasy in my wagon with so much iron—my guns, pistols, powder &c, but was not struck—altho' much exposed on a hill. The rain beat very hard against my carriage, & completely drenched my driver, sleeping under it, but I kept quite warm.

"Oct 10th weather changed—much cooler & rain still continues.... We made but little progress today, roads being very muddy & heavy—about 20 miles & reached Chouteau's Island in the evening which is about 80 miles from Bents Fort. It was so damp & wet, I did not get out on the ground at all today, but remained housed up in my carriage.

"Oct 11th Saturday Rain—Rain—

"Oct 12th Sunday Weather cold & damp. We travelled very hard today—the roads very muddy & heavy—the animals did not make much speed. Mr Bent being anxious to get on to the Fort, pushed ahead at any rate. In the night we started out again & made a few miles."

Anna Maria Morris traveled from Fort Leavenworth to Santa Fe in the summer of 1850. She rode with a party of U.S. soldiers commanded by her husband, Major Gouverneur Morris. Volume two of *Covered Wagon Women*, edited by Kenneth L. Holmes (Arthur H. Clark Company, 1990) *P*, contains Anna's diary of the trip. In it she had much to say about the hot weather:

"Friday June 14th Our journey to day was 22 miles & we are again encamped on the banks of the Arkansas—It has been very hot to day but in consequence of the high wind we have not felt the heat very much....

"Sunday June 16th The Thermometer at 98 [degrees] we have travelled 20 miles to day.... We expect to cross the Arkansas tomorrow— The heat to day is intolerable....

"Wednesday June 19th We have travelled 18 miles to day & are encamped at the first *water hole* after leaving the Arkansas—it is intensely hot, no wood, miserable grass, & only hot muddy water for the men & horses which they drink as tho' it was delightful—We had an awful wind storm this afternoon....

"Tuesday [June] 25th We have marched 15 miles to day [in] this sand, heat, & flies.... the heat *intense*—We passed a large pile of Mule sculls [skulls] to day. it is said 180 perished there last winter in the snow...."

Joseph Pratt Allyn traveled the Trail in 1863 on his way to Arizona. Letters he wrote along the way have been published in *West by Southwest, Letters of Joseph Pratt Allyn*, edited by David K. Strate (Kansas Heritage Center, 1984) *P*. By the time Allyn's caravan reached Colorado, winter weather had arrived:

"We were detained [at Fort Lyon] for four days, first for repairs and the necessity of rest, and last by a severe snow storm.... We passed the time comfortably in camp, barring a few frozen toes ... but it was difficult to avoid gloomy anticipations and forebodings with regard to the passage of the mountains as one looked at the shivering animals....

"On Friday, Oct. 30, we broke camp, the thermometer at zero at sunrise. It was no easy task to get up the frozen tents and get the train in marching order again. Coffee cooled on the way to your mouth, and handling tin places, cups, &c., seemed alike dangerous from heat and cold; I don't know which blistered the deepest.... But at last all the good-byes were said ... and over the crisp snow three or four of us galloped off in the piercing north wind, our beards frosted and our fingers benumbed."

In December 1852, James L. Collins, a Santa Fe newspaperman, wrote to the governor of New Mexico about the dangers of traveling the Trail in winter. His report, published in *On the Santa Fe Trail*, edited by Marc Simmons (University Press of Kansas, 1986) *P*, told about several blizzards:

"In the year 1851 the Cotton-wood Creek was again the scene of a terrible destruction of life. A Government train that had been started to the States by Col. Sumner, was overtaken by one of those destructive storms [and] in a single night nearly three hundred mules perished; one man was also lost, and several others badly frozen.

"In the same storm, the party in charge of the mail lost all their animals near Fort Atkinson, but [they] were picked up by [another] train."

Trail TRAVELER

Susan Magoffin

Long days, rough roads, stinging insects, bad weather—Susan Magoffin, the 18-year-old wife of a Santa Fe trader, experienced all those things during her trip down the Trail in 1846.

Susan Shelby Magoffin was born in Kentucky in 1827. She and her wealthy husband were living there when they decided to travel the **Trail**. Because Susan was expecting a baby, Mr. Magoffin provided her with as many comforts as possible: a "tent house," private carriage, books, "notions," a maid, driver, and at least two servant boys. Even so, the young wife suffered some discomfort while on the march.

Uncomfortable trip

Near the Little Arkansas River, swarms of mosquitoes made Susan miserable. According to her diary, "It was slap, slap, all the time . . . while the others came with a buz and a bite." Even though she slept under mosquito netting she was still covered with large red welts, "some of them quite as large as a pea."

At the Ash Creek crossing, Susan's carriage overturned on the steep stream banks. The damaged vehicle was a "perfect mess." Susan was shaken up but, except for a sore back and side, she seemed unhurt.

Two weeks later, she witnessed a prairie thunderstorm from the inside of a tent. "The lightning flashed its awful tongue in all directions, till the whole heavens seemed in one light blaze. The angry thunder raised its coarse notes, peal after peal. And the dark clouds, jealous[ly] . . . poured down the rain. The tent shook violently . . . and without a groan sunk to the flooded Earth!"

Bent's Fort

The Magoffins traveled by way of the **Mountain Route**. When they arrived at **Bent's Fort**, Susan described it as "my idea of an ancient castle." Built as a fortified trading post, the adobe outpost was a busy place. Traders, trappers, travelers, Indians, and Mexican employees visited or worked there. From her room near the courtyard, Susan heard "the shoeing of horses, neighing and braying of mules, the crying of children, the scolding and fighting of men."

The fort became "crowded to overflowing" when U.S. Army General Stephen Watts Kearny and 1,600 **infantry** troops camped nearby. The Mexican War had begun, and the American forces were on the way to New Mexico in conquest of new territory.

Susan celebrated her nineteenth birthday at Bent's Fort. The next day she gave birth to her baby. Perhaps because of her carriage accident, the child was born several months too early and it died. Susan spent 12 days resting before they continued on their way to Santa Fe.

To Santa Fe

The Magoffins spent five days crossing rugged Raton Pass. Susan walked or rode horseback through the roughest part. One day, she wrote, their wagons moved just "six or eight hundred yards." Going down a steep grade, it took six men "by bodily exertions," to pull wagons downhill—with their wheels locked.

The Magoffins arrived in Santa Fe in August. General Kearny and his forces had quietly taken control of Santa Fe a few days earlier. Susan, however, felt the city was anything but peaceful: "What an everlasting noise these soldiers keep up—from early dawn till late at night they are blowing trumpets, whooping like Indians, making unheard of sounds." She also noted in her diary that she was perhaps the first American woman in Santa Fe, and for years, historians believed that to be true.

After staying in Santa Fe for a time, the Magoffins took their **caravan** into Mexico. There Susan became ill with yellow fever and lost a second baby. She and her husband eventually returned to Kentucky, and then moved to Missouri. After her long journey, however, Susan was never well. She died in 1855 at the age of 28, after giving birth to a baby girl.

Mary Donoho was earlier

Historians have discovered that Mary Donoho, born in Tennessee in 1807, traveled the Trail with her husband and baby daughter in 1833—or 13 years earlier than Susan Magoffin. The Donohos ran a hotel in Santa Fe for four years. Their second daughter, Harriet, was born there in 1835. (She was possibly the first white child born in New Mexico.) After their son was born in 1837, Mary and the children returned to Missouri. The Donohos later moved to Texas. Mary died there in 1880.

Mary Donoho: New First Lady of the Santa Fe Trail (Ancient City Press, 1991) *P*, by Marian Meyer, tells more about Mary's life. Stella M. Drumm edited Susan Magoffin's Trail diary: *Down the Santa Fe Trail and Into Mexico* (University of Nebraska Press reprint, 1982) *P*.

A long day on the Trail

An ordinary day on the Santa Fe Trail was hard work for travelers and animals. Number these statements about a typical Trail day in the correct order. Use information from "On the march" (page 37) to help.

_____ If necessary, the wagons crossed a stream before stopping to make camp overnight.

_____ Crews rounded up animals, sorted, and hitched them to begin the morning march.

_____ Before the men ate their evening meal, they unhitched teams and took care of the animals.

_____ The cook or night herder woke the men.

_____ After their meal, the men made more repairs before they relaxed around the campfire.

_____ After eating, the men repaired wagons and harnesses, doctored animals, hunted, or did other necessary work.

_____ The animals were rehitched and the caravan traveled several more hours.

_____ About 10 A.M., the train stopped for a midday rest.

_____ Most men bedded down while the night herders and those on watch stayed awake.

_____ Men unhitched teams at the midday rest stop to let the animals drink, graze, and rest.

_____ The cook served the men their biggest meal of the day.

What do you think a day on the Santa Fe Trail might have been like? Write a diary page using your ideas.

A choice: mules or oxen

The two most common kinds of **draft animals** used on the Santa Fe Trail were mules and oxen.

Tough mules

After the first large group of mules was taken to Missouri from New Mexico in 1823, mules pulled more and more wagons on the **Trail**. Traders preferred them over horses because they were stronger, and ate less. A mule (a cross between a horse and a donkey) had a longer working life: 18 or more years, compared to about 12 years for a horse. Mules also got fewer saddle sores because of their tough hide and short hair. In most cases, it took only a short time to train a mule to pull a wagon.

But mules had their disadvantages. They were expensive. So were the leather harnesses and **running gear** (**singletrees** and **doubletrees**) that hitched them to wagons.

And they could be temperamental. Josiah Gregg once saw a stubborn mule leave furrows with its feet as the team dragged it along in its harness. Other times, mules ran at the "drop of a hat," remembered one **mule skinner**. His hat blew off in the wind, scaring his team—and soon the whole train stampeded. Another **teamster** recalled how a mule could stand on one leg and kick with the other three. "If I had my choice to work in a nitro-glycerine factory or to take care of a mule, I should go for the factory," he wrote.

Major Riley's experiment

Using oxen on the Santa Fe Trail came about almost by accident. In the spring of 1829, Major Bennet Riley was ordered out of Fort Leavenworth to protect a **caravan** headed to Santa Fe. Army funds wouldn't buy enough mules to pull the outfit's supply wagons, so the major decided to use some oxen. Not only were oxen cheaper, he reasoned, but they would need less feed since they could graze along the Trail. He also planned to butcher extra oxen for fresh beef.

The major's experiment worked well. Although Riley and his troops had to stop at the Mexican border (the Arkansas River west of modern Dodge City), he loaned a **yoke** of oxen to the caravan's captain, Charles Bent. Bent used the two oxen to pull a wagon on to Santa Fe and back. He found that the animals worked fine, except when their feet became tender. The next season Bent took an ox team of his own to Santa Fe.

Variety of 'bulls'

Oxen were usually called "bulls," even though they were all steers. Most oxen on the Santa Fe Trail were range cattle from Texas or the southeastern United States. They came in all colors, kinds, and sizes —but were lighter than the heavy oxen used in New England. The famous writer Horace Greeley described some Trail cattle at Leavenworth as "lean, wild looking oxen . . . of the 'long-horned' stripe."

Like Major Riley, many traders chose oxen because they were cheaper than other animals. In the 1840s, two oxen cost only $20 to $30. At the same time, a **span** of mules cost from $200 to $400, about the same price as horses. By the 1860s, a pair of mules cost $500 to $1,000, but oxen were about $150 per yoke.

Using oxen had other advantages. A wooden ox yoke was cheaper than leather harnesses for mules. Oxen's large hoofs pulled well through mud and sand. In emergencies, traders could eat the beef from oxen. And Indians didn't steal oxen as often as they stole horses or mules. The big, lumbering animals could not be ridden, they had no trade value with other tribes, and their beef was not appealing to Indians, who preferred buffalo meat.

Although oxen eventually outnumbered mules on the Trail, there were drawbacks to using them. They pulled slower than mules, and their hoofs often became tender. Some **bullwhackers** used metal ox shoes or tough leather ox "boots" to protect their animals' hoofs. Sometimes oxen got sick from cattle diseases or from eating poisonous plants.

In very hot weather, oxen did not work as well as mules. They did not always survive very cold weather, either. In 1850, one caravan lost 1,000 oxen when they died in a surprise blizzard on the Trail.

Why not horses . . . or camels?

Early Santa Fe traders used horses as pack animals, but freighters found the animals could not stand up to pulling heavy wagons day after day. Horses needed more to eat than just grass—but grain was expensive to carry along. Horses were also more sensitive to temperature, dust, and disease than mules and oxen. And, they were targets for Indian raiders. But wagonmasters, scouts, and others sometimes rode horses, so there were often some with a caravan.

Before the Civil War, the U.S. Army tried using camels as pack animals. Some of them could carry about 1,000 pounds, but the war and the humped creatures' bad tempers ended the experiment.

Wheelers, leaders, pointers

Whether using oxen or mules, traders hitched their teams in the same pattern. Use the bold words in the sentences below to complete these diagrams.

Traders hitched a pair of heavy, strong animals directly to the wagon. These **wheelers** did much of the pulling. They also carried the heavy wagon tongue, and helped hold the wagon back on steep downgrades.

The **leaders** led the team. Leaders were light, sure-footed, and intelligent animals. They set the pace for the whole team and directed the wagon.

A pair of **pointers** just ahead of the wheelers helped pull.

There were no seats on most freight wagons. A **mule skinner** rode on the nigh (left) mule of the wheeler pair. He guided the team with reins attached to the nigh mule in the leader pair.

Two or three pairs of **swingers** were hitched in front of the pointers. They were often the wildest and least experienced animals. It was their job to help turn the wagon.

A **bullwhacker** walked on the left side of his lead ox. He directed the animals by cracking a long bullwhip over their heads.

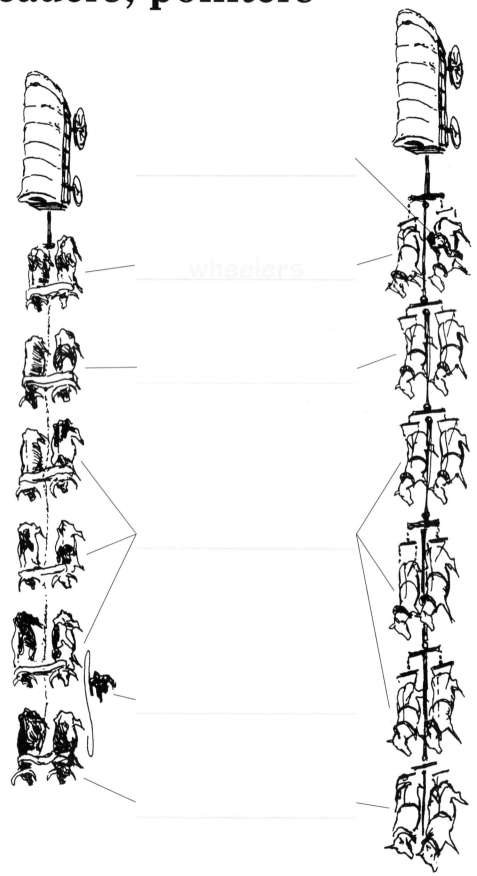

Spans of mules—or yokes of oxen?

Santa Fe traders faced a decision—which animals should pull their wagons. Use "A choice: mules or oxen" (page 41) to list some advantages and disadvantages of using both kinds of animals on the Trail.

Advantages

Advantages

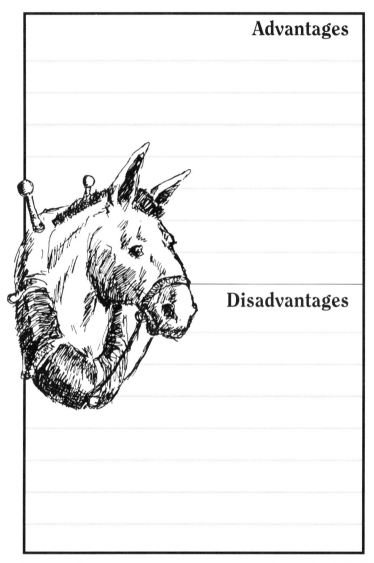

Disadvantages

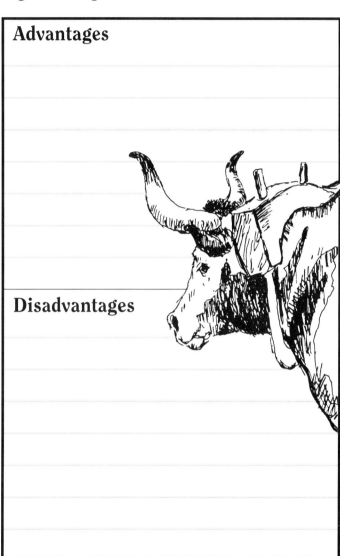

Disadvantages

For most traders, cost was the most important difference between animals. Compare costs in the 1840s and 1860s by using prices from "A choice: mules or oxen."

	1840s	1860s		1840s	1860s
One span of average-priced mules =	$	$	One yoke of average-priced oxen =	$	$
One team (6 spans) =	$	$	One team (6 yoke) =	$	$
One average-sized caravan (26 teams) =	$	$	One average-sized caravan (26 teams) =	$	$

Cost difference between wagon trains of mules and wagon trains of oxen = $ _____ $ _____

If you were a Santa Fe trader, which animals would you choose? Why?

Conestogas, J. Murphys

Some of the first Missouri traders traveled to Santa Fe with their goods loaded in farm wagons, "dearborns," or even two-wheeled carts, but most of those vehicles were too small to be practical. Dearborns were built for passengers and held just 500 pounds. Farm wagons with their narrow bodies and low sides held only 1,000 pounds. Larger wagons were needed for **Trail** traffic.

Conestogas from Pennsylvania

Through the 1840s, **Conestoga** wagons—sometimes called "Pittsburghs" or "Pennsylvanians"—were a popular Trail choice. They were a well-known brand of freight wagons built in Pennsylvania. (Many people called similar-looking wagons made by other companies Conestogas, too.) New Conestogas were shipped to Missouri by steamboat. Traders liked the large wagons because they carried about two tons of goods.

A cloth top made from canvas, cotton, or linen covered each Conestoga. The cover was stretched over several curved hoops, or bows. Conestoga wagon bodies were usually painted blue with bright red wheels and **running gear**. The **wagon bed** curved downward from the ends and sides, keeping freight from sliding as the wagon bounced along. With their curved bottoms and white covers, a **caravan** of Conestogas looked like a fleet of sailboats on wheels—or "prairie schooners."

Joseph Murphy's wagons

Of course other brands of wagons were used on the Trail, too. Traders bought Schlutter wagons made in Michigan, Studebakers made in Indiana, and wagons built by the many wagon makers who eventually operated in several Missouri cities.

One of the most popular St. Louis-built wagons was made by an Irish wagon maker named Joseph Murphy. He was a careful craftsman who used only strong woods like maple, hickory, and oak. He bored holes with hot irons instead of hand drills so the wood did not crack or rot around bolts. And he proudly stenciled "J. Murphy" on each wagon.

According to one story, Murphy wagons became popular in the early 1840s after Mexico began charging a $500 tax on every wagon brought to Santa Fe—no matter how large or small. When the tax was later dropped, traders continued to use J. Murphys because they were cheaper to operate than smaller wagons.

By the 1850s and 1860s, Joseph Murphy was making a wagon that could haul about 6,000 pounds. It had a body 16 feet long, a 50-foot tongue, and rear wheels that were seven feet tall. A man standing in the bed could not see over the sides!

Improvements in design

Over the years, wagon makers made improvements. They changed the design of the tongue to let it move up and down freely. This made it possible for wagons to cross streams with steep banks. To help wheels last longer, blacksmiths made iron tires that fit around the wooden rims. The rims were widened to eight or more inches to allow easier travel through sand. About 1845, wagon builders began using iron axles. The metal axles were much stronger, but more expensive than wooden ones. In the 1860s, wagons were redesigned so that freighters could hook two or more in **tandem** behind one team.

In the 1840s, traders paid about $130 for a Murphy wagon. Prices climbed as wagons were improved. By 1860 a large wagon cost from $800 to $1,500.

Breakdowns and brakes

On the rough Trail, any part of a heavily loaded wagon could break down. Traders carried hardwood to replace broken bows, axles, tongues, or spokes.

Wooden wagon wheels often dried out and shrank, causing the iron tires to fall off. Freighters then had to remove the wheels and soak them in a stream—if one was close by. Other times they hammered wedges between the rim and the tire. The best repair was to heat the tire until it expanded, slip the hot metal ring around the wheel, and shrink it tight against the wood with cold water.

To keep wagons from running away on downslopes, traders chained the rear wheels or put metal skids under them. Other times they fastened large logs under the backs of wagons to lift the rear wheels completely off the ground. Later, wagon wheels had brake shoes that the driver controlled with levers.

Trail schooner

Wagons built for use on the Santa Fe Trail had to stand up to rugged use. Although many of their parts were wooden (to save weight), most Trail wagons could carry 4,000 pounds or more. Match the bold words in the clues below with the missing labels on the wagon diagram.

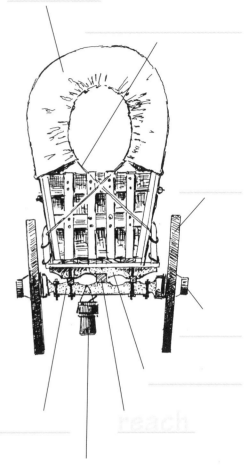

A wooden **wagon bed** or **box** was the body of a wagon. It had sloping sides and ends to keep freight from shifting on rough roads. A **tool box** filled with tools was mounted on the side of the bed. A **feed trough** hung on the back.

The top was covered with a cloth **cover** tied with a **drawstring**. The cover was stretched over curved **bows** made of hickory wood.

The undercarriage was supported by four wooden wheels. Each wheel had several parts: The outer rim was made of curved sections called **felloes**. Wooden **spokes** fit in the felloes and joined at the **hub**. An iron **tire** around the wooden rim protected it and held the wheel together. A driver stopped the wagon with levers that pressed a curved wooden **brake shoe** against each rear wheel.

The hub of each wheel turned on the end of a wooden **axle**. (Smart traders carried extras.) On top of each axle, a heavy **bolster** held up the wagon box. A long **reach** connected the two axles. The reach fit into a notch between each bolster and axle. Hanging from the rear axle was a **grease bucket** full of animal fat and tar to lubricate the hubs.

Animal teams were hitched to the **wagon tongue**. Ox yokes were fastened to the wooden tongue with chains; mule harnesses needed extra running gear.

45

Conflicts on the Trail

Several Indian tribes lived or hunted along the Santa Fe Trail. In eastern Kansas, the **sedentary** Osages and Kansas (Kaws) had permanent homes near some **Trail** sites. They raised corn, beans, and squash in gardens near their villages. Once or twice a year they traveled west to hunt buffaloes on the Plains. Pawnees also hunted near the Trail, even though they lived and farmed in Nebraska and northern Kansas.

Comanches, Kiowas, Southern Cheyennes, Southern Arapahoes, and Plains Apaches all hunted buffaloes in lands near the Santa Fe Trail. These **mobile** tribes ranged in present western Kansas, eastern Colorado, the Oklahoma Panhandle, and Texas. At times, some bands of Sioux also came into that area.

Farther southwest, Jicarilla Apaches, Utes, and members of several Pueblo tribes lived on lands near the Trail.

A clash of cultures

As the Santa Fe trade grew, trouble developed between Indians and traders because of differences in their cultures. Raiding had long been a way of life for the mobile tribes because they needed a constant supply of horses. Native American boys learned that stealing horses was a brave and honorable act. Young braves won respect for daring deeds in war. To the Plains tribes, slow-moving Trail **caravans** with hundreds of animals were easy raiding targets. Traders disagreed.

The first conflicts

On William Becknell's first wagon trip to Santa Fe in 1822, two of his men were trying to find several strayed horses when they met some Indians. The "rascally Osages," as Becknell called them, whipped his men, then took their horses, guns—and their clothes.

In 1825 the Osage and Kansa tribes signed treaties with the U.S. government. After that time, most of their clashes with traders were not serious, and the eastern end of the Trail was usually safe for travelers. The dangerous portion of the trip began near the Little Arkansas River. That was the beginning of buffalo-hunting country for Plains tribes.

In the early years of the Santa Fe Trail, however, meetings between traders and Indians were not always deadly. Indian parties sometimes visited caravans, poking inside wagons, tents, and anything else in camp. They tried to trade for ammunition, and begged or demanded food and gifts from nervous traders.

During the first six years of the trade, only three traders are known to have died in Indian attacks. But in 1828 the situation changed. Within just a few weeks, three more traders and over twice as many Indians were killed in fighting on the Trail.

In northeastern New Mexico that August, unidentified Indians shot two young scouts from a caravan as they slept beside a creek. Robert McNees died at the scene—and the location took his name: McNees Crossing. The other scout, Daniel Munroe, later died near the Cimarron River.

While traders were burying the bodies, a small party of Indians (possibly Pawnees) rode up. Out of revenge, the angry traders killed all but one of them, although the Indians probably knew nothing of the earlier attack.

Farther east, along the Arkansas River, Pawnees raided the same caravan and took about 700 horses and mules. A few weeks later, a smaller group of traders came upon a large Comanche camp near the Upper Cimarron Springs. The Indians attacked, killing and scalping John Means, captain of the party. The other traders slipped away in the night—and had to walk most of the way back to Independence.

Escorts for a caravan

Because of these **depredations**, Major Bennet Riley was ordered to escort the 1829 caravan, the first time American troops guarded wagons on the Trail. With Riley's 200 **infantry** soldiers along, the caravan was not

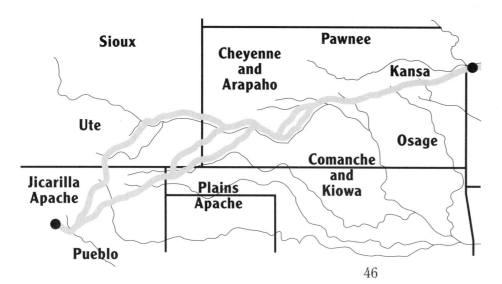

bothered by Indians—until it crossed the Arkansas River in western Kansas. The major was not allowed to travel beyond that point because land south of the river was part of Mexico. He and his men camped on the Arkansas' north bank to wait for the traders to return.

The caravan had gone less than ten miles into Mexican territory when about 50 Indians ambushed the **advance party**: Charles Bent, his younger brother William, and Samuel Lamme. Lamme was killed, but the Bents made it safely back to the train. They sent volunteers to get Major Riley, and he marched his troops across the river to rescue the caravan.

For five days, Riley escorted the nervous traders. But he then turned back. He was not authorized to take American troops into Mexico.

The traders were bothered by Indians most of the way to Santa Fe. In constant danger for nearly six weeks, they slept in their clothes and boots each night. Along the way, 120 Mexicans joined them. When they neared Taos, they were met by trappers who helped them finish their journey safely.

On their return trip, Mexican soldiers escorted the wagons to the Arkansas River, helping fight off another Indian attack on the way. (During his wait along the river that summer, Major Riley lost at least four men in Indian attacks, as well.)

The U.S. Army provided escorts for Santa Fe traders five more times before the Mexican War began. Because Riley's foot soldiers had a difficult time chasing mounted Indians, mounted troopers called **dragoons** were used on later trips. However, these escorts did not stop all the Trail violence.

Forts established

As more wagons crossed Indian lands, there were more chances for conflict. The Mexican War from 1846 to 1848 and the California gold rush in 1849 caused large increases in Trail traffic.

Up until that time the only fort near the Trail was Fort Leavenworth, about 30 miles northwest of Independence. It was established along the Missouri River in 1827. Fort Leavenworth followed Fort Osage, Missouri (used by troops at different times between 1808 and 1822).

In 1846 the Army built Fort Marcy in Santa Fe at the western end of the Trail. (Late that summer, the first **cavalry** troops on the Trail rode from Fort Leavenworth to Santa Fe.) The first military **post** actually on the Trail was Fort Mann, a handful of log buildings near the Cimarron Crossing of the Arkansas River. That post, built in the spring of 1847, was never more than a repair station and rest stop. The few troops there could do little to stop the Indian threat. Fort Mann was abandoned in 1848.

At that time, Lieutenant Colonel William Gilpin recommended that the Army construct four forts between the Pawnee Fork and upper Canadian River, and station troops at **Bent's Fort**, a trading post on the upper Arkansas. He estimated that Indians in 1847 had stolen 6,500 head of livestock, had destroyed 330 wagons, and had killed 47 men along the Trail.

Following Gilpin's suggestion, the government tried to buy Bent's Fort in 1849, but William Bent refused to sell it. He closed and destroyed much of his trading post that same year. (Construction on Bent's Fort was started about 1833. The adobe fortress sat on the north bank of the Arkansas near Timpas Creek. It was never an official U.S. Army post, although troops stayed there briefly during the Mexican War. Traders using the **Mountain Route** often rested inside its protective walls.)

Over the years the Army opened more Trail forts. In 1850 Fort Atkinson was built near old Fort Mann. It was in a good location to protect the Trail, but only a few troops were put there. The soldiers nicknamed it "Fort Sod" because of its sod buildings. (Field mice must have been a problem in the sod walls. In 1851 the commanding officer had a dozen cats shipped out from Fort Leavenworth!) Fort Atkinson was expensive to keep supplied because of its great distance from Fort Leavenworth. It was closed in 1854.

The Army built Fort Union, New Mexico, in 1851. It was near the western junction of the **Cimarron Route** and Mountain Route. Fort Union included a large supply depot to outfit other forts in the West. In Kansas, Fort Riley opened two years later. It sat along the Kansas River, near the Santa Fe and Oregon Trails. In 1859 Fort Larned was established near the mouth of the Pawnee Fork. Fort Lyon was built the next year along the Arkansas in eastern Colorado, downstream from Bent's Fort.

War on the Trail

The Civil War years were also dangerous times on the Santa Fe Trail. In the spring of 1862 Confederate troops took control of Santa Fe, but Union forces drove them out of New Mexico within a few weeks. Battles at Apache Canyon and Glorieta Pass (or Pigeon's Ranch) were two important Civil War conflicts that took place on the Trail.

At the same time, Indians seemed determined to close the Trail. Because many troops from forts in Kansas, Colorado, and New Mexico were moved east to fight Confederates, the Plains tribes may have believed they could drive whites out of their territory once and for all.

Fighting reached a peak in 1864. Wagons were held at Fort Larned and Fort Union until large caravans could be formed for protection. That summer the Army established Fort Zarah as an escort station just east of Walnut Creek. It was considered a branch of nearby Fort Larned until 1868. It was closed a year later.

More forts

With the end of the Civil War in 1865, the Army prepared for more fighting on the Trail. Troops were moved back on the Plains. Fort Dodge was established a few miles east of where Forts Mann and Atkinson had been located. Two small temporary posts were also opened: Camp Nichols was on the Cimarron Route in what is now the Oklahoma Panhandle (from May to November 1865). Fort Aubry was on the Mountain Route, near the north end of the Aubry Cutoff (from September 1865 to April 1866).

The Trail was quieter in 1865, apparently because of the extra troops. In 1866 the Army feared more trouble. Small trains were not allowed west of Fort Larned, but there was only minor fighting that season.

Caravans were again attacked during what has been called the 1867–68 Indian Wars. For several months (June to November 1867), cavalry troops were stationed at Camp Grierson. It was a temporary Trail post near an old stone corral at the crossing of the Little Arkansas River. The Army's tough winter **campaign** of 1868–69 finally forced most Plains tribes onto reservations. After that time, small Indian bands made only a few major raids on the Trail.

Seven military posts were left along the Santa Fe Trail in the 1870s. But, by the turn of the century, most were abandoned. The Army closed Fort Larned in 1878, Fort Dodge in 1882, Fort Lyon in 1889, Fort Union in 1891, and Fort Marcy in 1894. Soldiers are still stationed at Forts Leavenworth and Riley.

1864: A violent year

April—Kiowas attacked caravans and stole livestock near Fort Larned.

May—Cheyennes and Kiowas attacked stage stations near Fort Larned. A stage company employee was killed near Cow Creek.

July—Kiowas raided Fort Larned and stole 172 Army animals on the 17th. Two men died in a fight near Cow Creek. Two others were killed at the Cimarron Crossing.

August—Kiowas and Comanches attacked a caravan near Fort Lyon on the 7th. The next week, Comanches killed five men near Lower Cimarron Springs. They also stampeded stock from a wagon train. On the 19th, Indians burned wagons, stole livestock, and killed ten men near Cimarron Springs. Two days later, Indians attacked five caravans near old Fort Atkinson. They killed a wagonmaster and took several hundred animals.

September—On the 25th, troops from Fort Larned came upon a camp of about 4,000 Kiowas, Arapahoes, and Cheyennes on the Pawnee Fork. Two soldiers and nine Indians died in a fight that followed.

November—On the 29th, Colonel John Chivington and 700 troops attacked Black Kettle's camp north of the Trail in eastern Colorado. Over 150 Cheyennes and Arapahoes in the village on Sand Creek were killed. (While some of Black Kettle's men may have taken part in the spring and summer raids, two-thirds of the Indians killed in the massacre were women and children.)

Touring the Trail forts

Even though the U.S. Army closed most Santa Fe Trail forts over 100 years ago, modern Trail travelers can still visit some of them.

Bent's Fort and Forts Larned and Union are historic sites operated by the National Park Service. Fort Osage is a county museum. The Kansas Soldiers Home is at Fort Dodge; a veterans' hospital is at Fort Lyon. Still standing at both locations are buildings from Trail times. Forts Leavenworth and Riley are still active Army bases, and both have museum exhibits about the Trail.

The sites of most of the other Santa Fe Trail forts are marked with signs.

Trail VOICES
Indians

In the fall of 1858, David Kellogg traveled west on the Mountain Route of the Trail. The young adventurer hoped to strike it rich in a Colorado gold mine. In his diary, reprinted in *On the Santa Fe Trail*, edited by Marc Simmons (University Press of Kansas, 1986) P, Kellogg described meeting Indians along the Arkansas River:

"October 11th. While in camp at noon today a large band of Kiowas and Arapahoes came scurrying down the river banks on both sides, going on a buffalo hunt. They swarmed into our corral and insisted that we feed them as toll for passing through their lands. As we saw that they would eat us out of house and home we hurriedly hitched up and drove on. They were sullen and threatening because we could not continue feeding them....

"The Indian on his pony, clad in breech clout and moccasins, his copper-colored skin glistening in the sun, his head shaved except for a scalp-lock from which dangles an eagle feather, his face painted, riding up to the train with spear and shield of buffalo hide, sitting [on] his horse like a statue, straight as an arrow and as haughty as the Devil, he is the chief of wonders of this strange land.

"We trade sugar or coffee for buffalo robes. Pointing to the sugar or coffee, holding up a tin cup and extending five fingers and pointing to the robe is an offer of five cups of sugar or coffee for the robe. If accepted the Indian says, 'How, how.'"

James M. Fugate worked as a bullwhacker on the Santa Fe Trail in 1853. His Trail reminiscences have been reprinted in *On the Santa Fe Trail*. Here is how James described an Indian attack at Pawnee Rock:

"About 8 o'clock [in the] morning, just as we had brought our cattle up to the corral, and were yoking them up, a band of Cheyennes, to the number of about 300, suddenly made a dash from the north, . . . and immediately surrounded our corral of wagons, with a terrible war-whoop. Leaving our cattle just as they were . . . we instantly seized our weapons and pitched in vigorously to repulse the assault.

"The Indians opened a heavy fire from the start. They made strainers of our wagon-boxes by perforating them with bullets and arrow-heads. The Indians who were mounted fired high, and may possibly sometimes have hit some of their own men on the opposite side. . . .

"After firing in this way for a while . . . they beat a hasty retreat to the south, taking with them their dead and wounded. . . . In this fight we had one man wounded, and several cattle killed."

George Bent was the son of William Bent and his wife Owl Woman. He grew up at Bent's Fort, but during the Civil War he went to live with his mother's people, the Southern Cheyennes. Young Bent took part in several raids on the Santa Fe Trail and later wrote letters about his experiences. They were published in the book *Life of George Bent, Written from his Letters*, by George E. Hyde (University of Oklahoma Press, 1968) P. This is Bent's version of two raids near the Cimarron Crossing in the spring of 1867:

"As soon as the Cheyenne bands came together [from their winter camps], war parties were made up . . . as war had already been begun by [U.S. Army General Winfield Scott] Hancock [who had burned a large Cheyenne and Sioux village near Fort Larned].

"When we reached the [Cimarron] Crossing we found the skeleton of Lone Bear on the river bank. Eagle Nest had been killed by the soldiers back in the sand hills away from the river, but we could find no trace of his body. That evening we attacked a mule train going west and took about fifty head of mules.

"Next day we left the Arkansas and started west along the Cimarron route toward New Mexico. Soon we saw a mule train coming east. Our party hid in a ravine near a spring, or water hole, to wait until the mules were turned out to water and graze. . . . But, as so often happened, some of the warriors could not wait until the right time. They broke away from the rest of us and made a charge at the herd. The white bell [lead] mare saw them coming, instinctively turned and ran for the camp, and of course all the mules followed her. Our main party was still hiding in the ravine, but when we saw the mules turn we made a rush for the herd.

"The men with the train opened fire on us to turn us away from the mules; but we kept on and cut off twenty-two mules and four horses before the herd reached the wagons. Howling Wolf . . . made a rush for the white bell mare [but] before he could turn [her] he was shot through the thigh and gave up the chase.

"Two years later I met the boss of this train in Colorado and drank with him. He told me that this big wagon train had been hauling government supplies to Fort Union, and they were on their return trip east when our war party struck them."

Trail TRAVELERS

Franz and Ernestine Huning

Travel on the Santa Fe Trail was sometimes filled with danger, as merchant Franz Huning and his wife Ernestine found in 1867.

Franz Huning, born in Germany in 1827, came to America in 1848. After living in St. Louis for several months, he decided to head to the gold fields of California in 1849. With no team and wagon of his own, Franz joined a U.S. government **caravan** out of Fort Leavenworth. The young **greenhorn** soon found a job working as a **bullwhacker**.

Franz's caravan met Kansa Indians at Council Grove, but the meeting wasn't entirely friendly. He later wrote, "It appears that during our stay there, some of our **teamsters** killed a dog belonging to the Indians, for which the Indians afterwards revenged themselves when we were out on the road by charging up to the train and killing two of our oxen, calling out why they were doing it."

Once in New Mexico, Franz decided to stay there instead of going on to California. Eventually he owned a successful hardware business in Albuquerque. He made yearly **Trail** trips to buy merchandise in Kansas City and St. Louis.

On one of his visits to St. Louis, Franz met Ernestine Franke. She had been born in Bavaria in 1837 or 1838, and had immigrated to the United States with her family. The Hunings were married early in 1863, and that spring Franz took his new wife home to New Mexico.

Ernestine kept a diary of her journey, one of the few written records kept by a woman on the Trail.

Diary of a trip

Like Susan Magoffin, Ernestine traveled with servant help and "many comforts"—"china dishes, camp chairs, and a table." Early into the trip, her cook served "goose breast and truffles." Ernestine even brought along ten canaries.

Considering the dangers that lurked on the Trail during the Civil War years, the Huning party had a quiet trip. Except for several spring thunderstorms, they had no problems with weather. They traveled easily, their wagons often on the march by 4 or 5 A.M. One warm night, they drove by moonlight until 10 P.M.

To Ernestine, the Kansas prairie was "fresh and lovely, the foliage a beautiful green." She described part of the **Cimarron Route** as "an immense flower garden, the wild flowers so thick and lovely. . . . We can imagine ourselves in a park, though the refreshments are lacking."

The Indians they met seemed friendly. Near Cow Creek she wrote: "Some have their faces painted. All are tall, well built. They always beg, but are satisfied when they get something to eat, and go. We saw one of their houses made of branches with a hole in the middle for the smoke to go out."

In New Mexico she wrote: "Wooded hills make the scenery attractive; the stream coming down the rocks rushes like a river. This afternoon we have a wonderful view in front of us. As far as we can see are snow-covered mountains which reach into the white clouds, and lower down [are] forests."

Sad news

Unfortunately, Franz's Trail trip wasn't as pleasant four years later. In the spring of 1867 he took five wagons east to St. Louis on his annual buying trip. He then went on to Ohio, where he met Ernestine's mother and younger brother Fritz. They had come from Europe to join the Hunings in New Mexico.

As Franz and his relatives traveled back west on the Trail, their caravan was attacked by Indians near Plum Buttes in central Kansas. It began, according to Franz's account, "when all at once one of the teamsters at the rear end of the train called, 'Indians, Indians!' At first I could not see them on account of a dense growth of high sun flowers along the road and as they made no noise in the grass and soft sandy soil."

In the fighting that followed, the Indians killed Mrs. Franke, Fritz, and their driver, and burned several wagons. Franz escaped to nearby Fort Zarah, where he wrote letters to Ernestine telling of the sad news.

The Hunings continued to live in Albuquerque. In later years, Franz owned a ranch and a flour mill. In the 1880s he and Ernestine built an elaborate home nicknamed "Castle Huning." It was there that he died in 1905. She also died in Albuquerque, in 1923.

Franz's recollections of Trail days were published in *Trader on the Santa Fe Trail*, edited by his granddaughter, Lina Fergusson Browne (The University of Albuquerque, 1973). Ernestine's Trail diary appears in *On the Santa Fe Trail*, edited by Marc Simmons.

Trail TRAVELER

Little Raven

Little Raven was a Southern Arapaho leader who grew up in the territory of the Santa Fe Trail. He ranged over the Plains during his lifetime, probably crossing the Trail many times. And as the road to Santa Fe became busier, it certainly affected his life.

Little Raven was born about 1817 near the Platte River, in what is now Nebraska. As a young man he was known for his intelligence and speaking ability. By 1840 he had married a Kiowa-Apache woman, probably the first of his seven wives. (An Arapaho man often married the younger sisters of his wife, or the wives of a brother who died.)

About the same time, he helped arrange a council at which the Southern Arapahoes and Southern Cheyennes made peace with the Kiowas, Kiowa-Apaches, and Comanches. With their wars ended, most **mobile** tribes turned their attention to **depredations** on the busy Santa Fe Trail. During the violence, Little Raven often spoke for peace.

Treaties and broken promises

When his father died in 1855, Little Raven became the principal chief of the Southern Arapahoes. On a visit to Denver, he ate his hosts' food, smoked their cigars, and explained that he liked white men. He was glad to see them getting gold, he said, but he hoped they would soon leave his people in peace. In 1860 he attended peace talks held near **Bent's New Fort** and was given a medallion showing the face of President James Buchanan. The chief proudly wore his medal until he later lost it. Then he was so upset he offered ten horses to anyone who found it.

For a time, Little Raven became unhappy with the white men's broken promises and he joined the Cheyennes' war parties. Later, however, he spoke out strongly for peace, even after some Arapahoes were killed in two **campaigns** against Cheyennes: Colonel John Chivington's 1864 raid on Chief Black Kettle's camp at Sand Creek, Colorado —and Lieutenant Colonel George Custer's attack on the Cheyenne chief's new village in Indian Territory (Oklahoma) four years later.

Little Raven signed treaties in the 1860s that left the Arapahoes with only a small reservation—located first in eastern Colorado, and then in Indian Territory.

At treaty talks along Medicine Lodge Creek in 1867, Little Raven was described as "good-natured." He greeted some of the peace commissioners with such big hugs that they were smeared with his face paint. During those Kansas meetings, he invited reporters and other whites to a tribal dance. When a gun was stolen from one of his guests, Little Raven offered one of his own Colt revolvers to replace it.

'De-tailed' ponies

Robert Wright remembered a humorous incident with Little Raven on the **Trail**, before the Southern Arapahoes moved to Indian Territory. Wright, a stagecoach driver at the time, had to leave a large Concord coach stuck in the mud west of Fort Larned. As he was riding on to the **post**, he met Little Raven and some of his band. Wright asked them to haul the coach to the fort, and the chief agreed.

Sometime later Little Raven appeared at Fort Larned—but without the stagecoach. He had left it 20 miles up the Trail, he told Wright, and "blessed if he could get it any farther." With no harnesses, the Indians had tied their ponies to the heavy vehicle—and had pulled the hair out of nearly every one of the poor animals' tails!

Speaking for peace

Along with a group of Plains tribal chiefs, Little Raven traveled to the East in 1871 to meet government officials. During a speech in New York, Little Raven gave an Indian's view of white settlement and travel on the Santa Fe Trail:

"Long ago the Arapahoes had a fine country of their own. The white man came to see them, and the Indians gave him buffalo meat and a horse to ride on, and they told him the country was big enough for the white man and the Arapahoes, too.

"After a while the white men found gold in our country. They took the gold and pushed the Indian from his home. I thought Washington would make it all right [but] the Government sent agents and soldiers out there to us, and both have driven us from our lands. We do not want to fight. We want to travel the same road as the white man. My people are waiting in the hills to greet me when I return, and I want to give them a good report."

Chief Little Raven returned to the reservation. Following his advice, the Arapahoes kept out of the Indian wars in the 1870s. He died in the winter of 1889 at Cantonment, Oklahoma, after many years as a respected leader of his tribe.

Scouting the Trail forts

Identify the 14 Santa Fe Trail military posts—and Bent's Fort—on this map. Use location clues from "Conflicts on the Trail" (pages 46–48).

Fort Mann and Fort Atkinson share the same numbered symbol because they were located so close together.

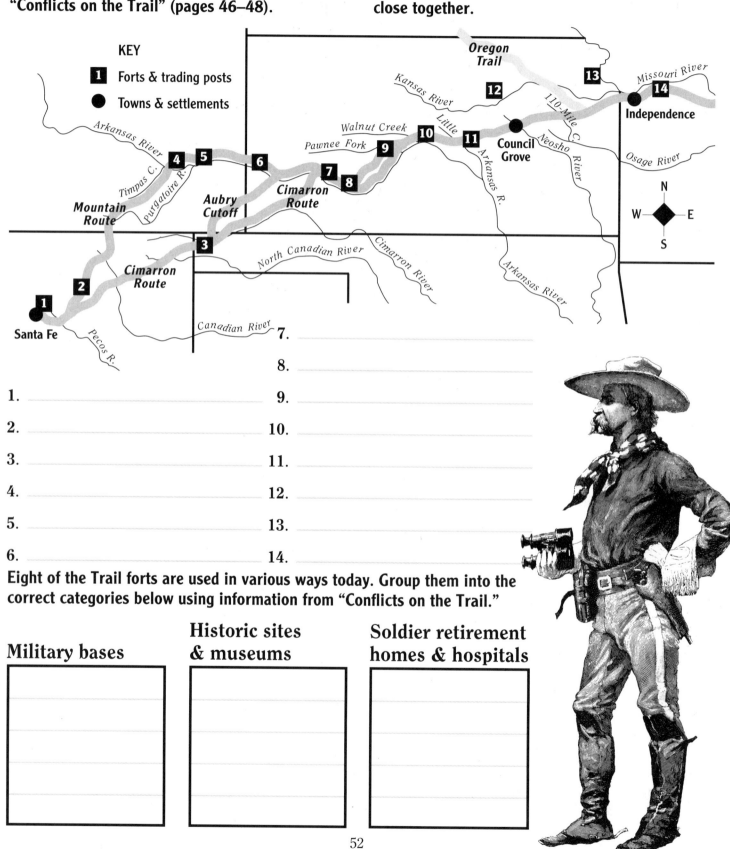

1. _____
2. _____
3. _____
4. _____
5. _____
6. _____
7. _____
8. _____
9. _____
10. _____
11. _____
12. _____
13. _____
14. _____

Eight of the Trail forts are used in various ways today. Group them into the correct categories below using information from "Conflicts on the Trail."

Military bases

Historic sites & museums

Soldier retirement homes & hospitals

Trail forts, 1808–1900

As the Santa Fe trade grew, the number of Trail forts increased. While you read "Conflicts on the Trail" (pages 46–48), finish the table at right. Write the names of the Trail's 14 military posts and the years each was open. Include Bent's Fort, too.

Then complete the timeline below. First, list the forts in the order they were established. Next, shade the years each post was in operation.

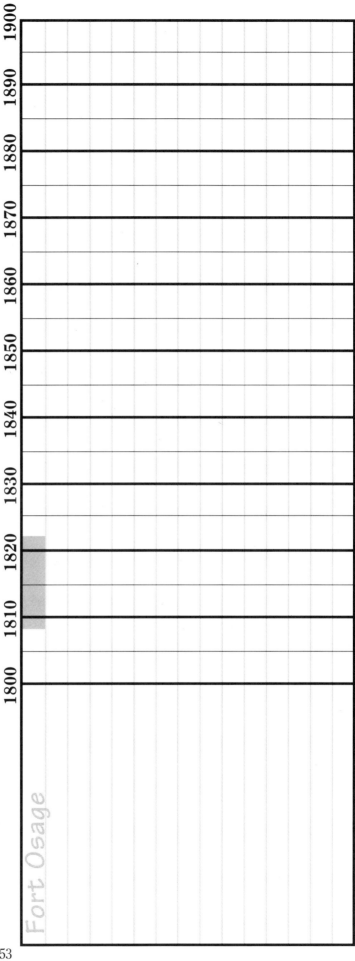

Conflicting stories

How do historians learn about events and people from the past? When possible, they use original sources of information: letters, diaries, photographs, newspapers, reports, or other documents.

But sometimes, historical accounts don't agree. That is the case with the story of a fire on the Santa Fe Trail, May 19, 1868. Who burned the Fort Zarah trading post that night? And why? Although archaeologists have uncovered some clues at the site, the mystery is still unsolved. Read the evidence. What do you think?

On the night of Tuesday, May 19, 1868, a mysterious fire destroyed Joseph W. Douglass' trading post on the Trail. The sandstone building was located at the Walnut Creek crossing, just east of present Great Bend, Kansas. Nearby was Fort Zarah, a small military post established in 1865.

At the time of the fire, Douglass' building was the **sutler's** store at the fort. It was also part of a **road ranch** operated by the trader. (The ranch was originally built by William Allison in 1855.) Like other road ranches on the Trail, the Walnut Creek ranch was a place for travelers to eat and drink, spend the night, purchase goods, and buy, sell, or trade livestock.

Indians also came to the ranch, and exchanged furs and buffalo robes for supplies. Charles Rath, the trader who operated the store before Douglass, was forced to leave Fort Zarah in 1867 because he was selling guns, ammunition, and whiskey to Indians. It isn't known if Douglass was involved in any such illegal trade.

At the time of the fire, Cheyennes, Arapahoes, Kiowas, and Comanches were camped north and south of the Trail between Fort Dodge and Fort Larned, waiting for goods and **rations** to be given out by their Indian agents. Even though several thousand Indians were in the camps along the Trail, no one had reported any **depredations** against travelers that spring.

On Thursday, May 21, the commander at Fort Larned, Captain Nicholas Nolan, 10th U.S. Cavalry, mentioned the trading post fire in the letter below.

(In these letters, the information inside brackets [ ] has been added to explain the writers' words. Information left out of the original documents has been replaced with three dots . . . called an ellipsis.)

"That between the hours of 10 and 11 PM 19th inst. [instant, meaning "of this month"] the ranche near Fort Zarah Ks . . . was burned by a party of Indians evidently Cheyennes

"Mr Douglas[s] . . . had been warned of the intentions of the Indians, by a letter from Ed[mond] Guerrier and took refuge in the Garrison [Fort Zarah] Everything was quiet at Zarah on the morning of the 20th inst"

On Sunday, May 24, this account of the trading post fire was published in a Leavenworth newspaper, the *Daily Commonwealth*:

FROM THE PLAINS!

INDIAN OUTRAGES!

A TRADING POST BURNED!

We gain the following intelligence from Mr. Joseph Douglas, who has just arrived here from the West. Some months ago Mr. Douglas was appointed Post Trader by the commanding officer at Fort Zarah, and his store was on Walnut Creek, very near that Post. On Tuesday last, the 19th, about one hundred and twenty five Cheyennes, accompanied by a few Arapahoes, came to the trading house and demanded whiskey. They were refused, and became very much excited. It was evident, from their manner, that they had already been drinking. Not succeeding in their efforts, they resorted to all possible schemes to provoke a collision with the white men and the soldiers. They cocked revolvers and held them at the heads of white men. Holding their revolvers in this way, some of them compelled soldiers to take cartridges and bury them in the sand, and then dig them up again. Lieut. Shepherd is in command at Fort Zarah, but he has only twenty five men, and if they had resented any of the insults heaped upon them, it would have resulted in an indiscriminate massacre of the entire garrison. Matters went on in this way all Tuesday afternoon, the Indians occasionally galloping up the Creek to obtain whisky from some miscreant who was thus feeding them with fire.

In the evening Mr. Douglas left his store and went to the Fort. At about ten o'clock the Indians were seen kindling a fire around the store, and in a few minutes the building was in flames. The store and all its contents—valued at $5,000—were entirely destroyed. The Indians then went away.

The general feeling in that vicinity is that the Indians mean to fight. They recently told a white man named Parker, with whom they claim to be friendly: "When we go down to Zarah, look out! every white man is a ―――." They drew fifteen sacks of flour at Larned, the other day, and then threw it away.

It is plain that it will take only a spark to kindle this excited mass into a flame which will spread all over the Plains.

On Monday, May 25, Captain Nolan reported more on the fire to his regional headquarters at Fort Harker, Kansas:

"On the afternoon of the 19th inst a party of Cheyenne Indians came [to] Fort Zarah Ks. and proceeded to Mr Douglas ranche & desired to trade with him, but having nothing with them for that purpose. They showed an insolent disposition [disrespectful attitude] but offered no violence during the day

"On the same night about 9 OClock the Indians went into Mr T[–?–]'s ranche distance 1/2 mile from Mr Douglas and asked for something to eat which having obtained they departed and were seen no more. Between 10 & 11 OClock the same night Mr Douglas ranche was fired [burned] while he and Mr [Parker ?] were inside[.] they fled from the ranche and sought protection in the garrison[.] On the next day 9 bullet holes were found in the door evidently fresh & fired from the outside

"It is believed the ranche was fired by the Cheyennes from personal motives of hatred toward Mr Douglas

"The above report has been delayed in order to obtain full particulars [details] from Fort Zarah Ks"

Major E.A. Belger at Fort Harker apparently received the report that same day, and he immediately wrote to the commanders at Fort Dodge and Fort Larned:

"It is reported at these Headquarters, that a certain Edward Geary [Edmond Guerrier] who lives with the Cheyennes, either at Forts Dodge or Larned, wrote a note to Mr. Douglass at Fort Zarah, advising him to treat a certain party of Cheyennes with kindness, to give them crackers, &c. This note was received by Mr. Douglass prior to [before] the burning of his store on the night of the 19th inst. by Cheyennes, as stated.

"The fact that this store alone was burned, no lives taken, and no other outrage committed, while there was every chance to destroy much more property, looks strange for the work of Indians alone.

"The Commander . . . therefore directs that you will endeavor to attain through Mr. Geary or others, the reasons why this attack was made. . . . It will be advisable to keep this matter quiet until you get the necessary information."

Two weeks later, on June 8, the new commander at Fort Larned, Captain Henry Asbury, 3rd U.S. Infantry, answered Major Belger's letter:

"I would respectfully report, in reply to communication dated . . . May 25th 1868, that I have seen Mr Guerrier, and he states that his intention in writing the note to Mr Douglas, telling him to treat the Indians with kindness was, that [Douglass] might get what little trade the Indians might have to give him

"The night the ranche was burned, there were but two Indians absent from camp, and in [Guerrier's] opinion [they were] not in the direction of Mr Douglas' ranche at all[.] He says Mr Douglas made no attempt to save his property or goods. It is Mr Guerrier's opinion that it was not the work of Indians, but that of white men."

Edmond Guerrier was a trusted scout and interpreter who often worked for the U.S. Army. He was the son of a French trapper and a Cheyenne woman, and was married to William Bent's half-Cheyenne daughter Julia. Edmond and Julia were living with her Cheyenne relatives at the time of the fire.

Joseph Douglass was a Civil War veteran who had been held prisoner by the Confederates. (He weighed just 67 pounds when released.) Two months after the fire on Walnut Creek, he moved to Butler County, Kansas. There he chose the location of a new town—Douglass. Joseph was the community's first postmaster and "one of the most public-spirited men in the county." According to a U.S. government record of "Indian Depredation Claims," on August 26, 1868, he asked for $5,445 to pay for merchandise destroyed by Cheyennes on May 19. It isn't known if Douglass collected any money for the claim before he died in 1872.

In May 1969, the Kansas State Historical Society and the Kansas Anthropological Association excavated the site of the Walnut Creek road ranch. They uncovered remains of a large sandstone structure, about 80 by 20 feet. Thomas Witty, the archaeologist in charge, believed it was the trading post that burned in 1868.

At the north end of the building they found broken dishes, pieces of furniture, gun parts, and other items that suggested it was a living area that had burned with all its furnishings. The south two-thirds of the structure appeared to have been one large storeroom. But when archaeologists excavated that whole area they found a surprise: the room was empty—except for a pile of large nails. Was Douglass' storeroom empty at the time of the 1868 fire? That was difficult to prove 101 years later, but Witty believed no "treasure hunters" had removed artifacts over the years, because the soil at the depth of the original floor was undisturbed when the archaeologists dug into it.

Whose version of the fire was printed in the newspaper?
Who felt the cause of the fire should be investigated? Why?
Which evidence pointed toward Indians being guilty? Which did not?
Who had a reason to say the Cheyennes were innocent? Why?
Who might have burned the trading post besides Indians? Why?

Trail places

If you would like to experience the Santa Fe Trail in person, here are some places to visit.

National historic sites and monuments

Fort Larned, Kansas
Bent's Old Fort, Colorado
Fort Union, New Mexico
Pecos Pueblo, New Mexico

Other museums

MISSOURI
Lexington Historical Museum, Lexington
National Historic Trails Center, Independence
Harry S. Truman Library and Museum, Independence
Raytown Museum, Raytown
Kansas City Museum of History and Science, Kansas City
John Harris House, Kansas City
John Wornall House, Kansas City
Alexander Majors House, Kansas City

Beginning in the early 1900s, the Daughters of the American Revolution placed granite markers along the Trail (except in Oklahoma). Many of these DAR markers can still be seen.

KANSAS
Old Castle Museum, Baldwin City
Kaw Mission State Museum, Council Grove
United States Cavalry Museum, Fort Riley
Adobe House Museum, Hillsboro
McPherson County Museum, McPherson
Coronado-Quivira Museum, Lyons
Barton County Museum, Great Bend
Santa Fe Trail Center, Larned
Sod House Museum, Kinsley
Boot Hill Museum, Dodge City
Grant County Museum, Ulysses
Santa Fe Trail Museum, Ingalls
Finney County Museum, Garden City
Kearny County Museum, Lakin
Hamilton County Museum, Syracuse

COLORADO
Big Timbers Museum, Lamar
Koshare Indian Museum, La Junta
Baca-Bloom Houses and Pioneer Museum, Trinidad

NEW MEXICO
Old Aztec Mill Museum, Cimarron
Seton Museum, Cimarron
Kit Carson House, Rayado
Santa Fe Trail Museum, Springer
City Museum, Las Vegas
Governor Bent House and Museum, Taos

National historic landmarks

MISSOURI
Arrow Rock
Fort Osage

KANSAS
Fort Leavenworth
Mahaffie House and Farmstead, Olathe
Council Grove
Pawnee Rock, Pawnee County
Trail ruts west of Dodge City
Wagon Bed Springs, Grant County

OKLAHOMA
Camp Nichols, Cimarron County

NEW MEXICO
Clayton Complex, Union County
  McNees Crossing
  Rabbit Ears Mountain
  Round Mound (Mount Clayton)
Raton Pass, Colfax County
Wagon Mound, Mora County
Fort Union
Watrous
Pecos Pueblo
Glorieta Pass, Santa Fe County
Plaza and Palace of the Governors, Santa Fe
Kit Carson House, Taos

Other landmarks

Cave Spring, Jackson County, Missouri
Blackjack State Park and Trail ruts, Baldwin City, Kansas
Lost Spring, Marion County, Kansas
"Ralph's Ruts," Rice County, Kansas
"Charlie's Ruts," Kearny County, Kansas
Chouteau's Island site, Kearny County, Kansas
Middle Spring, Morton County, Kansas
Point of Rocks, Morton County, Kansas
Point of Rocks, Finney County, Kansas
Point of Rocks, Colfax County, New Mexico
San Miguel, New Mexico

Today, signs with this official logo mark the route of the Santa Fe National Historic Trail and certified historic sites along it. The signs were placed in cooperation with the National Park Service.

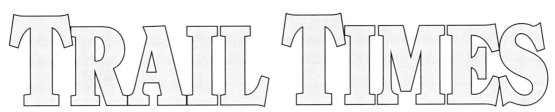

VOLUME I   ON THE SANTA FE TRAIL   **NUMBER 1**

Published and edited by

Trail books

Younger readers might enjoy the Santa Fe Trail books on this page marked with a star.* Titles in print are marked P. Other Trail books are mentioned throughout this book.

Samuel Hopkins Adams,
The Santa Fe Trail *
(Random House, 1951)

Larry M. Beachum,
William Becknell: Father of the Santa Fe Trade (Texas Western Press, 1982)

Erick Berry,
When Wagon Trains Rolled to Santa Fe * (Garrard Publishing Company, 1966)

Wyatt Blassingame,
Bent's Fort: Crossroads of the Great West * (Garrard Publishing Company, 1967)

William E. Brown,
The Santa Fe Trail (The Patrice Press, 1988) *P*

William Y. Chalfant,
Dangerous Passage: The Santa Fe Trail and the Mexican War (University of Oklahoma Press, 1994) *P*

Seymour V. Connor and Jimmy M. Skaggs,
Broadcloth and Britches: The Santa Fe Trade (Texas A&M University Press, 1977)

Glen Dines,
Bull Wagon * (Macmillan, 1963)

R.L. Duffus,
The Santa Fe Trail (University of New Mexico Press reprint, 1972)

Gregory M. Franzwa,
Images of the Santa Fe Trail * (The Patrice Press, 1988) *P*

Gregory M. Franzwa,
The Santa Fe Trail Revisited (The Patrice Press, 1989) *P*

Mark L. Gardner,
Brothers on the Santa Fe and Chihuahua Trails (University Press of Colorado, 1993) *P*

Mark L. Gardner, editor,
The Mexican Road: Trade, Travel, and Confrontation on the Santa Fe Trail (Sunflower University Press, 1989) *P*

Mark L. Gardner,
Santa Fe Trail: National Historic Trail * (Southwest Parks and Monuments Association, 1993) *P*

Holling Clancy Holling,
Tree in the Trail * (Houghton Mifflin Company, 1942) *P*

Henry Inman,
The Old Santa Fe Trail (Corner House Publishers reprint, 1977) *P*

David Lavender,
The Santa Fe Trail * (Holiday House, Inc., 1995) *P*

David Lavender,
The Trail to Santa Fe * (Trails West Publishing reprint, 1986) *P*

Gene and Mary Martin,
Trail Dust * (Johnson Publishing Company, 1972) *P*

Edith McCall,
Heroes of the Western Outposts * (Childrens Press, 1960) *P*

Edith McCall,
Wagons over the Mountains * (Childrens Press, 1961) *P*

Dan Murphy and Bruce Hucko,
Santa Fe Trail, Voyage of Discovery * (KC Publications, 1994) *P*

Joan Myers and Marc Simmons,
Along the Santa Fe Trail (University of New Mexico Press, 1986)

Leo E. Oliva, editor,
Adventure on the Santa Fe Trail (Kansas State Historical Society, 1988) *P*

Leo E. Oliva,
Fort Larned (Kansas State Historical Society, 1982) *P*

Leo E. Oliva,
Soldiers on the Santa Fe Trail (University of Oklahoma Press, 1967)

Leo E. and Bonita M. Oliva,
Santa Fe Trail Trivia * (Western Books, 1989) *P*

Dorothy L. Pillsbury,
Star Over Adobe * (University of New Mexico Press, 1963)

Jack D. Rittenhouse,
Trail of Commerce and Conquest, A Brief History of the Road to Santa Fe (Santa Fe Trail Association, 1987) *P*

Marc Simmons,
Following the Santa Fe Trail (Ancient City Press, 1986) *P*

T.J. Sperry,
Fort Union: A Photo History * (Southwest Parks and Monuments Association, 1991) *P*

Ross McLaury Taylor,
We Were There on the Santa Fe Trail * (Grosset & Dunlap, 1960)

Robert M. Utley,
Fort Larned: National Historic Site * (Southwest Parks and Monuments Association, 1993) *P*

Robert M. Utley,
Fort Union and the Santa Fe Trail (Texas Western Press, 1989) *P*

Henry Pickering Walker,
The Wagonmasters (University of Oklahoma Press, 1966) *P*

David N. Wetzel, editor,
The Santa Fe Trail: New Perspectives (Colorado Historical Society, 1987) *P*

Bookin' on down the Trail

Book title:

Author:

Some facts I learned about the Trail:

Trail terms

advance party A group of scouts who traveled ahead of a **caravan**.

Aubry Cutoff The shortcut on the Santa Fe Trail laid out by Francis X. Aubry in 1851. It left the **Mountain Route** several miles west of Upper Crossing and joined the **Cimarron Route** between Upper Spring and Cold Spring. Aubry's cutoff had a better supply of grass, water, and wood than the **Jornada** section of the Cimarron Route. Sometimes misspelled *Aubrey*.

Bent's Fort or **Bent's Old Fort** The large adobe trading post built in the 1830s by William and Charles Bent and their partner Céran St. Vrain. It was located on the **Mountain Route** of the **Trail** along the Arkansas River. Because William Bent destroyed most of it in 1849 and later built **Bent's New Fort**, it is often called Bent's Old Fort. Also called Fort William.

Bent's New Fort The stone trading post on the Santa Fe Trail built by William Bent in 1853. It was on the Arkansas River about 40 miles downstream from the first **Bent's Fort**. The U.S. government leased it in 1860 but later abandoned the site.

buffalo (or **cow**) **chips** Dried manure that was burned for fuel.

bullion [BOOL-yon] Gold or silver shaped into bars instead of coins.

bullwhacker A wagon driver who drove oxen. Bullwhackers walked on the left side of their lead animals and controlled them with a bullwhip.

Caches [KASH-ez] Storage pits that were a **Trail** landmark along the Arkansas River just west of present Dodge City. (They disappeared many years ago.) The Baird and Chambers trading party spent the winter of 1822–23 in that area after most of their animals died in a blizzard. In the spring they dug large pits in the side of a nearby hill and cached, or stored, their goods while they went to Taos to buy more animals. Indians, explorers, traders, and pioneers often used caches to store food and other goods. From the French word *cacher*, meaning "to hide."

campaign A military operation. Along the **Trail**, campaigns were almost always aimed at Indians.

caravan A group of traders and their wagons traveling together.

cavalry [KAV-ul-ree] Soldiers trained to fight on horseback.

Cimarron Route or **Cimarron Cutoff** The Santa Fe Trail route first used by William Becknell in 1822. It began at the Arkansas River and ran through southwestern Kansas, the western edge of the Oklahoma Panhandle, and northeastern New Mexico to near Fort Union. The Cimarron Route was shorter, but drier than the **Mountain Route**.

Chouteau's Island [SHOW-toes] An island landmark that was once in the Arkansas River southwest of present Lakin, Kansas. (The island washed away many years ago.) It was named for Frenchman Auguste P. Chouteau who was in a group of trappers that took cover there during a fight with Pawnees in 1816.

commerce [KOM-urse] The buying and selling of goods.

Conestoga [KON-us-TOE-guh] A popular brand of covered wagon manufactured in Pittsburgh, Pennsylvania. Many similar-looking wagons built by other wagon makers were also called Conestogas.

contraband [KON-truh-BAND] Goods not allowed to be imported or exported; often items that a government considers dangerous.

depredations [DEP-ruh-DAY-shuns] Attacks or robberies. Many depredations in **Trail** days were carried out by Indians.

doubletree A crossbar on a wagon to which two animals' **singletrees** are fastened.

draft animals Animals used to pull wagons, plows, or other heavy loads.

dragoon [druh-GOON] An **infantry** soldier also trained to fight on horseback. In the U.S. Army, dragoons were replaced with **cavalry** soldiers.

dry goods Cloth, clothing, and other similar trade items.

Dry Route One of two Trail routes between **Pawnee Rock** and Fort Dodge. It was called dry because it was several miles north of the Arkansas River. It was less sandy than the **Wet Route**.

dugout A shelter or home dug into the side of a hill. Dugouts often had roofs made of sod blocks laid on a support of tree branches or lumber.

greenhorn A person who is new to a job and has no experience. Also called a tenderfoot.

infantry [IN-fun-tree] Soldiers trained to march and fight on foot.

Jornada [hor-NAW-duh] The part of the **Cimarron Route** between the Arkansas River and the Cimarron River where travelers often had a difficult time finding water. From the Spanish word *jornada*, meaning "a day's journey." Also called the Cimarron Desert.

leaders A pair of **draft animals** hitched at the front of a team.

loopholes Small holes or slits in a wall through which weapons can be fired.

mess A group of people, often in the military, who regularly eat meals together; the place where such meals are served; a meal.

mobile Indians that lived in tipis and hunted buffaloes. They moved several times a year, often north in the summer and south in the winter. Mobile tribes along the Santa Fe Trail were the Kiowas, Comanches, Southern Cheyennes, Southern Arapahoes, Plains Apaches, Sioux, Jicarilla Apaches, and Utes.

Mountain Route or **Mountain Branch** The route of the Santa Fe Trail that followed the Arkansas River into eastern Colorado to near **Bent's Fort**, and then southwest along the eastern edge of the Sangre de Cristo Mountains. It joined the **Cimarron Route** near Fort Union. Also called the Bent's Fort Route and the Raton Route.

mule skinner A wagon driver who drove mules and controlled them with reins. Mule skinners usually rode the left **wheeler** mule.

nigh An old-fashioned term for left. Bullwhackers walked on the nigh side of their lead pair of oxen.

notions Sewing items such as needles, thread, buttons, and ribbons.

Pawnee Rock A landmark in Kansas between the Big Bend of the Arkansas River and the mouth of the Pawnee Fork River. It is a hill with a red sandstone face that **Trail** travelers could see for many miles. Its name came from a battle that was fought nearby between Pawnee and Comanche Indians.

Point of Rocks Rocky landmarks that are visible for many miles. Several sites on the Santa Fe Trail are named Point of Rocks: one in New Mexico, one in Colorado, and two in western Kansas. (A third Kansas Point of Rocks was destroyed in 1981 to make room for a highway.)

pointers A pair of **draft animals** in the middle of a team hitched just ahead of the **wheelers**.

post Another word for fort or trading post.

Rabbit Ears A mountain and a nearby large flat-topped hill in eastern New Mexico. From some places on the **Trail**, this landmark looks like the tips of a rabbit's ears on the horizon. Some say it was named for Rabbit Ears, a Cheyenne chief who was killed in that area by Spaniards.

railhead The farthest point on a railroad to which track has been laid.

ration [RASH-un or RAY-shun] An amount of food allowed for a person.

relief A group of people who share guard duty.

revolt To rebel against those in authority.

road ranch A trading post on the **Trail** where the owner also often bought and sold livestock. Also spelled *ranche*.

running gear The working parts of a wagon (wheels, axles, etc.) or other vehicle.

sedentary [SAID-in-TARE-ee] Indians that lived in permanent homes (made of mud, adobe, or grass), raised crops (corn, beans, and squash), and made several trips a year to hunt buffalo. Sedentary tribes that lived or hunted near the Santa Fe Trail included the Kansas (Kaws), Osages, Pawnees, and several groups of Pueblos.

singletree A crossbar to which one animal is harnessed. A singletree, in turn, is fastened to a **doubletree** on a wagon. Singletrees, doubletrees, and harnesses are needed to hitch mules to a wagon; oxen are hitched with only **yokes** and chains.

sowbelly Bacon preserved with salt. Also called salt pork.

span A pair of **draft animals** working together. On the Santa Fe Trail a span usually meant two mules.

sutler A merchant allowed by the military to set up a store at a fort and sell supplies to soldiers.

swingers A pair of **draft animals** hitched just behind the **leaders**.

tandem [TAN-dum] When two or more wagons are fastened together and pulled by one team.

teamster A wagon driver. See **bullwhacker** and **mule skinner**.

terrain [tur-RAIN] Type of land: hilly, level, mountainous, etc.

toll road A road that one must pay a toll, or fee, to use. In the 1860s Richens "Uncle Dick" Wootton built a toll road over Raton Pass that was used by travelers on the **Mountain Route** of the Santa Fe Trail.

Trail A course or route between two points. In this activity book, Trail with a capital *T* always refers to the Santa Fe Trail.

trailhead The beginning of a trail. As railroads built west, the Santa Fe Trail had different trailheads. Also called a jumping-off point.

wagon bed The body of a wagon where cargo is carried. Also called a wagon box.

wagonmaster The leader of a wagon train or **caravan**. Also called the trail boss.

Wagon Mound A small mountain in New Mexico near the junction of the **Cimarron Route** and the **Mountain Route**. It looks like a covered wagon being pulled by oxen.

Wet Route The route of the Santa Fe Trail along the Arkansas River between **Pawnee Rock** and Fort Dodge. It was called wet because it followed the river. It was a sandier road than the **Dry Route**.

wheelers A pair of **draft animals** in a team hitched directly to a wagon.

yoke A pair of **draft animals** working together; or the wooden bar used to hitch two animals to a wagon. On the Santa Fe Trail a yoke usually meant two oxen.

Trail terms practice

How many Trail terms have you learned? Match words from the list at the bottom of the page with the meanings below. "Trail terms" (pages 60–61) will help. Use three of the words from the list to identify the pictures at right.

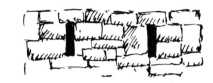

_____ The buying and selling of goods.

_____ Attacks or robberies.

_____ Soldiers trained to fight on foot.

_____ Soldiers who fight on horseback.

_____ Another word for wagon train.

_____ The leader of a wagon train.

_____ A beginner or tenderfoot.

_____ A pair of animals, often mules.

_____ A teamster who drove mules.

_____ A teamster who drove oxen.

Complete these sentences with Trail terms from the word list below.

The Trail runs through hilly land in Kansas; near Santa Fe it runs through mountainous _____.

To travel over a _____, one has to pay a fee.

At different times, Franklin, Arrow Rock, Independence, and Westport were _____.

At the store run by the _____ at Fort Larned or Fort Union, one could buy _____ and _____.

Instead of paper money and coins, some traders were paid in _____.

One team could pull two wagons when they were hitched in _____.

Everyone working in a caravan received a daily food _____.

Word list

caravan	dry goods	mule skinner	span	toll road
cavalry	greenhorn	notions	sutler	trailheads
bullion	commerce	infantry	ration	tandem	wagonmaster
bullwhacker	depredations	loopholes	singletree	terrain	yoke

62

Conestoga crossword

Across

1. Trail boss
5. New Mexico landmark that looks like a team and wagon (*2 words*)
7. Arrow Rock and Independence are in _____
11. Popular brand of wagon made in Pittsburgh, Pennsylvania
13. Chihuahua and Mexico City are in _____
14. State with the most Trail mileage
15. Type of Indian tribes such as Kiowa, Comanche, Cheyenne, and Arapaho
16. Famous Colorado trading post (*2 words*)
17. A pair of oxen
18. Group of people who regularly eat together
19. Storage pits that became Trail landmarks
23. First U.S. military fort built *on* the Santa Fe Trail (*2 words*)
24. Kansas landmark named for Indians (*2 words*)
26. Kansas town where caravans organized (*2 words*)
27. Caravans traveled about 15 _____ a day
30. Spanish nickname for the Journey of Death
31. Type of Indian tribes such as Osage, Kansa, and Pawnee
32. Trade goods such as needles and thread
33. "Uncle Dick" Wootton built a toll road over _____ (*2 words*)
34. Popular St. Louis wagon builder (*2 words*)

Down

2. Trail route that crossed Raton Pass (*2 words*)
3. What ended wagon traffic on the Trail
4. Father of the Santa Fe Trail (*2 words*)
6. War that gave the U.S. control of New Mexico (*2 words*)
8. Another name for the Cimarron Route (*2 words*)
9. Cattle used as draft animals on the Trail
10. Waterway that the Mountain Route followed into Colorado (*2 words*)
12. Ox driver
13. Mule driver (*2 words*)
20. Bacon preserved with salt
21. Trade goods such as nails and tools
22. Draft animals that were tougher than horses, but were sometimes stubborn
25. Trade goods such as cloth and clothing (*2 words*)
27. New Mexico creek and crossing named for a young man murdered there in 1828
28. The city at the western end of the Trail (*2 words*)
29. A pair of mules

A table of Trail travelers

Choose some of the people from the "Trail traveler" pages in this book—or Trail travelers from other sources—and complete this table with information about them.

Trail traveler	Born when and where	First traveled the Santa Fe Trail when and why	Died when and where

Quick quiz

Nothing but nouns! Mark the people, places, and things listed below that were part of the history of the Santa Fe Trail.

___ religious pictures
___ sacks of flour
___ Federal Express drivers
___ longhorn steers
___ pots and pans
___ Santa Fe Railroad trains
___ Conestoga wagons
___ Point of Rocks
___ runaway teams
___ Mohawk Indians
___ the "Last Chance" store
___ axes
___ the Grand Canyon
___ Comanche Indians
___ mule skinners
___ sewing notions
___ broken wagon axles
___ Long Island R.R. trains
___ kegs of nails
___ loggers
___ Pueblo Indians
___ U.S. mail coaches
___ Kiowa Indians
___ infantry soldiers
___ Cimarron River Wal-Mart
___ Thomas Jefferson
___ Mexican traders
___ cloth
___ the Great Salt Lake

Who's who? Match each Santa Fe Trail character with the correct clue from the list below.

___ Kit Carson
___ Marion Russell
___ Francis X. Aubry
___ Alexander Majors
___ William Mathewson
___ William Bent
___ Susan Magoffin
___ Antonio José Chávez
___ William Becknell
___ Joseph Murphy

A. built popular Trail wagons.
B. ran a Trail road ranch; was the first to be called "Buffalo Bill."
C. set several Trail speed records.
D. was the first to use wagons on the Trail.
E. was murdered on the Trail in Kansas.
F. believed workers should follow Christian rules.
G. first traveled the Trail as a child; later lived at Camp Nichols.
H. ran popular trading posts on the Trail.
I. believed she was the first white woman to travel the Trail.
J. was a famous mountain man, scout, soldier during Trail days.

Before and after... Mark the Trail event that happened first in each of these sentence pairs.

___ The Mexican War. [or]
___ The Civil War.

___ The Trail became a Nat'l Historic Trail. [or]
___ The railroad reached Santa Fe.

___ Forts were built up and down the Trail. [or]
___ Becknell traded in Santa Fe.

Where in the world? In which states would you find these Santa Fe Trail sites today?

Camp Nichols,

Fort Larned,

Wagon Mound,

Independence,

Fort Osage,

Santa Fe,

Bent's Fort,

Pawnee Rock,

Council Grove,

Fort Union,

Rabbit Ears,

Franklin,

Trail review

What do you remember about the history of the Santa Fe Trail? Fill in the correct answers.

Route

The Santa Fe Trail was a route that connected the state of **1.** _____ on the east with what is now the state of **2.** _____ on the west. The state with the most miles of the Trail is **3.** _____, while the state of **4.** _____ has the least Trail mileage. The other Trail state is **5.** _____.

Early history

In 1821, **6.** _____ became the first American to trade successfully in Santa Fe. The next year, he returned to Santa Fe, driving the first **7.** _____ over the Trail. Because of this, he is known as the **8.** "_____."

Cargoes

Four items that traders took to Santa Fe were:

9. _____
10. _____
11. _____
12. _____.

Four items that traders hauled from Santa Fe were:

13. _____
14. _____
15. _____
16. _____.

Conflicts

As traffic to Santa Fe increased, trouble developed between Indians and traders. Even though the U.S. Army built forts on or near the Santa Fe Trail, Indian tribes such as the **17.** _____ and **18.** _____ still raided in the area. During the **19.** _____ War, the United States took control of Santa Fe and new territory in the West.

Later history

By the end of the **20.** _____ War in 1865, several thousand wagons a year traveled the Trail. Other people and vehicles using the Trail (besides traders and freight wagons) were:

21. _____
22. _____
23. _____
24. _____.

However, things changed in 1880 when the first **25.** _____ arrived in Santa Fe. After nearly 60 years, the wagon days of the Trail ended.

Match these Santa Fe Trail characters, places, and terms with the correct definitions.

____ Kit Carson
____ caravan
____ mule skinner
____ Fort Union
____ Pawnee Rock
____ William Bent
____ commerce
____ bullwhacker
____ Fort Leavenworth
____ Conestoga
____ Wagon Mound
____ Bent's Fort

A. a popular Trail wagon made in Pennsylvania
B. a famous New Mexico Trail landmark
C. an ox driver
D. a wagon builder in St. Louis
E. a large fort near the Trail that is still an active U.S. Army base
F. a famous Kansas Trail landmark
G. was known along the Trail as a scout, soldier, and mountain man
H. ran popular trading posts on the Trail
I. took the first wagons over the Trail
J. an important Trail fort in New Mexico with a large supply depot
K. a mule driver
L. a fort along the Cimarron River
M. a group of traders and their wagons traveling together
N. the buying and selling of goods
O. an important trading post on the Trail

Match these names with the numbers on the Trail map.

____ Oregon Trail
____ Aubry Cutoff
____ Colorado
____ Fort Osage
____ Cimarron Route
____ Cimarron River
____ Fort Larned

____ Missouri River
____ Arkansas River
____ Missouri
____ Santa Fe
____ New Mexico
____ Council Grove
____ Franklin
____ Wagon Mound
____ Pawnee Rock

____ Fort Union
____ Oklahoma
____ Camp Nichols
____ Bent's Fort
____ Kansas
____ Mountain Route
____ Independence
____ Fort Leavenworth
____ Raton Pass

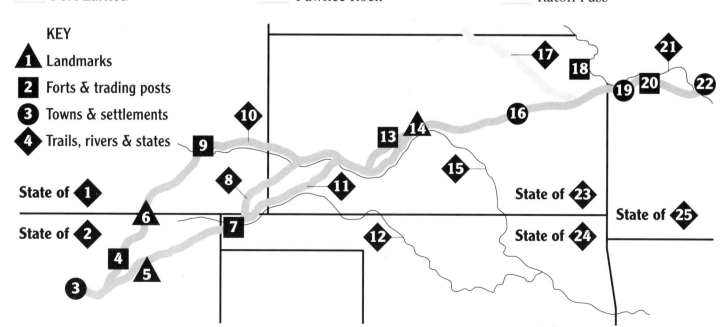

KEY
1 Landmarks
2 Forts & trading posts
3 Towns & settlements
4 Trails, rivers & states

Digging deeper

For more adventures with the Santa Fe Trail, try some of these projects. Most are based on pages in this activity book.

Pages 4–6—Learn more about the history of the Trail by joining the Santa Fe Trail Association. You can hear programs and meet other Trail fans at SFTA meetings. Read about all the latest Trail news in *Wagon Tracks*, the SFTA's quarterly newsletter. You can get information on how to join the association by writing:

Santa Fe Trail Association
Route 3
Larned, Kansas 67550

Page 7—Read Josiah Gregg's description of wagon trains and imagine you are watching a caravan as it leaves Council Grove or arrives in Santa Fe. What do you see? What sounds do you hear? What things can you smell? touch? taste? List or draw your ideas.

Pretend you are a television or radio reporter at the scene of George Vanderwalker's stampede or Matt Field's runaway wagon. Record your comments on audio or video tape.

Write a paragraph describing how you might have celebrated your birthday on the Trail in the 1800s.

Page 8—Calculate Francis X. Aubry's average speed per hour on his three record-breaking rides. Divide the distance he rode (about 770 miles) by the number of hours it took. How long would it take to drive the length of the Trail at 55 mph (without stopping)?

Follow Aubry's trips up and down the Santa Fe Trail using the index to *The Beginning of the West* by Louise Barry (Kansas State Historical Society, 1972). This book is an annals, or a chronology of events. It has many, many listings about the Santa Fe Trail and traders. Through its index you can track other Trail travelers and locate events that happened along the Trail.

Pages 10–11—Copy the timeline bar on page 71 on another sheet of paper and draw your own timeline of Trail history. Here are some events you might add: the years the five Trail states were admitted to the Union, the year your hometown was founded, the birth and/or death of some of the Trail travelers in this book, and other dates from this book or other sources.

Page 12—Use "A Trail into history" (pages 4–6) and encyclopedia articles to find different flags that could have flown at these locations: Santa Fe, Camp Nichols, Bent's Old Fort, Pawnee Rock, Wagon Bed Springs (on the Cimarron Route in Kansas), and Franklin. Remember, the flags shown on page 12 are modern.

Page 13—What other Spanish words do you recognize on the list? Do you know Spanish words that aren't listed? Use some of them in a paragraph, or sort them into categories.

Find words on the list that are spelled the same in Spanish and English. These words (like *actor* or *ángel*) are called "exact cognates." Even though exact cognates look alike and mean almost the same thing, they are often pronounced differently. Words that are spelled nearly the same and have similar meanings are called "cognates."

Locate Spanish place names (like Río Grande, Pueblo, Castaneda, and Cimarron) in the five Trail states. These books will be helpful:

William Bright,
    Colorado Place Names
    (Johnson Books, 1993) **P**

Sondra Van Meter McCoy and Jan Hults,
    1001 Kansas Place Names (University Press of Kansas, 1989) **P**

T.M. Pearce,
    New Mexico Place Names (University of New Mexico Press, 1994) **P**

Robert L. Ramsay,
    Our Storehouse of Missouri Place Names (University of Missouri Press, 1973) **P**

George H. Shirk,
    Oklahoma Place Names (University of Oklahoma Press, 1974) **P**

Ask a person who speaks Spanish to teach you the Spanish names for *wagon, ox, mule, caravan, cargo,* and other Trail-related words. Put the words you learn in your own Spanish dictionary.

Page 19—The mileage distances in the "Bent's Fort mileage" box on the next page were published in the *Westport Border Star*, January 28, 1859. Compare the figures with Josiah Gregg's figures on page 19. Which Trail route was measured? What was the beginning point? How do the names of the campsites compare with those on Gregg's table? How do these mileage distances compare on both tables: 110-Mile Creek to the Arkansas River? Diamond Spring to [Big] Cow Creek?

Using a modern highway map, find as many of the campsites from the *Border Star* chart and/or Gregg's chart as you can. Use the map's scale of miles and a ruler to measure the distance between several points. Do your figures agree with Gregg's and the *Border Star*'s?

Find the average distance between points on Gregg's table and the points on the *Border Star* table.

Write questions for friends or classmates to answer using the *Border Star* distance table.

Bent's Fort mileage

Miles between points

From Westport
- Brush Creek 2
- U.S. Mail Station No. 1 4
- Indian Creek 6
- Bull Creek 20
- Black Jack Point 10
- Willow Springs 11
- Palmyra 3
- Rock Creek 6
- Bone Yard 7
- 110-Mile Creek 4
- Burlingame 8
- Dragoon Creek 5
- Soldier Creek 2
- Chicken Creek 6
- Logchain Creek 2
- Elm Creek 2
- 142-Mile Creek 3
- Bluff Creek 7
- Rock Creek 8
- John's Creek 5
- Council Grove 2
- Elm Creek 8
- Diamond Spring 16
- Lost Spring 13
- Little Muddy Creek 10
- Cottonwood 7
- Running Turkey 19
- Big Turkey 8
- Big Muddy 15
- Little Arkansas 3
- Chaves [Chávez or Jarvis] Creek . . 9
- Owl Creek 4
- Little Cow Creek 2
- Big Cow Creek 3
- Big Bend of Arkansas 17
- Allison's Ranch 6
- Pawnee Rock 16
- Ash Creek 6
- Pawnee Fork 6
- Forks of Santa Fe Road 6
- Arkansas River 75
- Gunnison's 1st Camp 2
- 2nd Camp 19
- 3rd Camp 20
- 4th Camp 22
- 5th Camp 24
- 6th Camp 21
- Big Timbers 7
- 7th Camp 13
- Trading Post 1
- 8th Camp 12
- Purgatory Creek 3
- 9th Camp 12
- Bent's Fort 3

Pages 20–24—To fit the four Trail maps together at the same scale, copy pages 22 and 23 at 100%, page 21 at 71%, and page 24 at 105%. You may have to vary the percentages slightly on your copy machine.

List the counties crossed by the Trail in each state. Use the place name books on page 68 to research the origin of the names. Are any of the counties named for Trail travelers?

Using state maps, list highways and railroads that follow the Santa Fe Trail (and other trails) in your state. How are the modern routes different from the trails? Do you think the highways along the Santa Fe Trail have heavier traffic than other highways? On which of the railroad routes do passenger trains run?

Page 28—Buy Trail goods using the blank "Invoice" below. Choose items from the list on page 28 or the "Prices" box at right. Both sets of prices are based on goods Mariano Yrissarri bought in St. Louis in 1853.

Prices   page 28

coffee	$ .10 per pound
chocolate	.22 per pound
cinnamon sticks	.43 per pound
nutmeg	1.40 per pound
sweets	3.00 per box
preserved fruit	.42 per piece
almonds	.13 per pound
biscuits	4.25 per keg
sugar	.06 per pound
rice	.06 per pound
sugar cones	.08 per pound
soap	.05 per pound
sardines	.29 per can
honey	.60 per gallon
frijoles	.80 per bushel
brown sugar	.04 per pound
sassafras	3.00 per sack
candle wicks	.22 per pound
candles	.13 per pound
matches	1.00 per gross
percussion rifles	5.00 each
flintlock rifles	4.00 each
percussion caps	.05 per hundred
powder	5.00 per barrel

Invoice   page 28

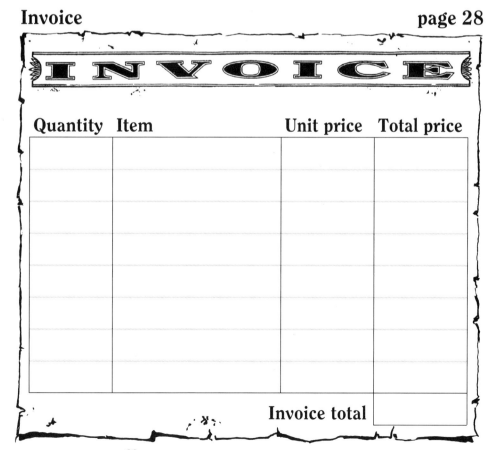

Page 29—Use Josiah Gregg's information to draw two more graphs: "Trail goods, 1833–1843" and "Wagons and men to Santa Fe, 1822–1832." Which kinds of graphs would best show this information: line, bar, circle, or picture graphs?

Page 30—Make a crossword, find-a-word, or another type of puzzle using the list of J.J. Webb's trade goods or the items bought by Mariano Yrissarri (see pages 28 and 69).

Page 31—Alphabetize the list of J.J. Webb's trade goods, or group them in two categories: items we use today and items that are obsolete. Can you think of other categories in which to group them?

Page 32—Keep a record of everything you eat for one day, and compare it with the daily food ration for Trail hands. Which diet is better balanced, yours or the Trail hand's? What items in today's food pyramid are missing from a Trail hand's diet?

Page 35—Use the total from the activity on page 35 (four weeks' wages) to figure the total wages for one round trip of a wagon train between Missouri and Santa Fe. An average caravan spent about eight weeks on the road to New Mexico, and about six weeks returning—depending on the type of draft animals used, and the weather. What other things could have affected the amount of time a caravan spent on the Trail?

Page 36—Choose another article in this book and create an outline of the important facts from it.

Page 38—List the disadvantages and discomforts of traveling the Trail in different types of weather. How do we avoid these problems when traveling today? Which types of weather would you have wanted to travel in during Trail days?

Use the index to Louise Barry's *Beginning of the West* to research weather events on the Trail up to the early 1850s. Which kinds of weather were people most likely to write about in Trail days?

Research to find the average annual precipitation along the Trail. These books will be helpful:

Warren A. Beck and Ynez D. Haase, *Historical Atlas of New Mexico* (University of Oklahoma Press, 1989) ***P***

John W. Morris, Charles R. Goins, and Edwin C. McReynolds, *Historical Atlas of Oklahoma* (University of Oklahoma Press, 1986) ***P***

Thomas J. Noel, Paul F. Mahoney and Richard E. Stevens, *Historical Atlas of Colorado* (University of Oklahoma Press, 1994) ***P***

Milton D. Rafferty, *Historical Atlas of Missouri* (University of Oklahoma Press, 1982) ***P***

Homer E. Socolofsky and Huber Self, *Historical Atlas of Kansas* (University of Oklahoma Press, 1988) ***P***

Page 43—Estimate the total cost of outfitting a 26-wagon caravan with animals and wagons in the 1860s. Start with the total cost for mules and oxen (1860s) from the activity on page 43. Then add these costs:

Wagons, $800 to $1,500 each in the 1860s, (see "Conestogas, J. Murphys," page 44).

Wagon covers, about $7.50 each, one per wagon.

Harnesses (mules only), $30 to $60 for each animal—twelve mules per wagon.

Yokes (oxen only), $1.25 to $2.25 for each pair of animals—six pairs of oxen per wagon.

Ox chains (oxen only), about $2.50 for each pair of animals—six pairs of oxen per wagon.

To find a "grand total" for wagons, animals, and men's wages, add the total you just calculated to the total trip wages you calculated in the page 35 project at left. What other expenses would a trader have had if he took a caravan to Santa Fe and back?

Pages 46–48—Use *Forts of the West* by Robert W. Frazer (University of Oklahoma Press, 1965) ***P*** or the place name books on page 68 to find the origin of the names of the Santa Fe Trail forts. Did any of those persons for whom forts were named actually travel the Trail?

Page 49—Draw a picture of the Indian that David Kellogg described.

Write an account of the James M. Fugate raid as if you were an Indian who had taken part. Write a short account of the raid George Bent described—from the point of view of the wagonmaster of the caravan.

Page 52—The clues in the "Trail forts" box on the next page will help you locate the Santa Fe Trail military posts on the map on page 52.

Pages 54–55—Rewrite one of the letters, correcting the original writer's capitalization, punctuation, and spelling mistakes. You could also correct mistakes in the "Trail voices" articles (pages 7, 38, and 49).

Page 56—If it's difficult for you to visit one of these Trail places, do your traveling by mail. Write for Trail information from the chamber of commerce in a Trail town, or exchange letters with students from a school near the Trail. What historic sites near your home could you tell about in your letters?

Page 57—Create a newspaper page about a visit to a Trail site. Include news stories and headlines. Draw a picture or a map in the box.

Page 59—Read a Trail book and complete the "Bookin' it" activity to tell others what you learned.

Trail forts — page 52

Fort Leavenworth was established on the Missouri River northwest of Independence.

Fort Osage was the only Santa Fe Trail fort in Missouri.

Fort Marcy was in Santa Fe.

Fort Mann was near where the Trail's Cimarron Route crossed the Arkansas River and headed toward the Cimarron River.

Bent's Fort was a trading post on the Arkansas River, near the mouth of Timpas Creek.

Fort Atkinson was built very near the spot where Fort Mann once stood.

Fort Union was on the Trail's Mountain Route, not far from its junction with the Cimarron Route.

Fort Riley was built along the Kansas River, between the Santa Fe and Oregon Trails.

Fort Larned was near the mouth of the Pawnee Fork.

Fort Zarah was near the mouth of Walnut Creek.

Fort Lyon was built along the Arkansas River in eastern Colorado, just downstream from Bent's Fort.

Fort Dodge was established a few miles east of where Forts Mann and Atkinson once stood.

Camp Nichols was on the Cimarron Route in what is now the Oklahoma Panhandle.

Fort Aubry was on the Mountain Route, near the north end of the Aubry Cutoff.

Camp Grierson was located where the Trail crossed the Little Arkansas River.

Page 60—Draw pictures, diagrams, or maps to illustrate some of the Trail terms.

Page 63—The words in the "Conestoga crossword" box below will help you solve the puzzle on page 63. There are three extra words.

Pages 65–67—Review what you've learned about the Trail by having a scavenger hunt with friends or classmates. Divide into teams and write questions for each other based on information in this book.

Page 66—The words in the "Trail review" box below will help you answer the questions on page 66. There are more than enough correct answers to fill all 25 blanks, plus ten extras.

Conestoga crossword — page 63

mess	dry goods	William
Mexico	Arkansas River	Becknell
yoke	Joseph Murphy	Kansas
sowbelly	hardware	railroad
mules	terrain	Wagon Mound
miles	Conestoga	oxen
span	Pawnee Rock	Santa Fe
Missouri	Mountain Route	Spain
mobile	Mexican War	Fort Mann
contraband	bullwhacker	tandem
caches	Council Grove	Raton Pass
notions	wagonmaster	Bent's Fort
Jornada	mule skinner	sedentary

Trail review — page 66

hardware	train	New Mexico
miners	furs	Navajo
Mohawk	Plains Apache	buffalo robes
soldiers	stagecoaches	Pueblo
Kiowa	adventurers	jewelry
donkeys	travelers	Osage
horses	Grover Cleveland	camels
Texas	Comanche	wool
Sioux	religious objects	Kansas
Missouri	Oklahoma	Kansa
wagons	Arapaho	canal
Mexican	Colorado	Civil
bananas	Jicarilla Apache	blankets
priests	dry goods	mules
gold	Cherokee	Ute
nuns	sewing notions	trappers
Nebraska	highway	mail wagons
Cheyenne	Pawnee	settlers
William Becknell	Father of the Santa Fe Trail	Spanish silver

1820
1830
1840
1850
1860
1870
1880
1890
1900
1910

1610–1848

The Trail's history stretches back to the earliest days of Santa Fe. Use the timeline to answer these questions about the Trail's past.

Santa Fe is the oldest American city west of the Mississippi River. How old is Santa Fe this year?
386 yrs in 1996

How many years was Santa Fe a Spanish city?
211 years

How many years was Santa Fe a Mexican city?
27 years

Who was the first American to trade legally in Santa Fe?
William Becknell

What happened that year that made his successful trade possible?
Mexican Rev. ended

How many years were some members of the McKnight-Baird trading party kept in jail?
9 years

What route did William Becknell use to travel to Santa Fe in 1822?
Cimarron Route

Number these persons in the order they first arrived in Santa Fe.
- **3** Stephen Watts Kearny
- **1** Zebulon Pike
- **2** William Becknell

Fort Mann was built **20** years **(after)** before Leavenworth was established.

1849–1987

Through the 1860s, the Santa Fe Trail was a busy road. Use the timeline to answer these questions about the history of the Trail.

Number these Trail forts in the order they were established:
- **3** Fort Lyon
- **5** Fort Aubry
- **1** Fort Union
- **2** Fort Larned
- **4** Fort Zarah

Fort ___ closed **13** years **(before)** after Fort Union closed.

Circle the fort that was open the greatest number of years.
Fort Dodge **(Fort Larned)**

Fort Union was open **40** years.

Where did people "rush" to in 1859?
Colorado [gold mines]

In what year were two Civil War battles fought on the Trail?
1862

Who built a road over Raton Pass?
[Uncle] Dick Wootton

What happened 14 years after the AT&SF Railroad reached Santa Fe?
Fort Marcy closed

How many years has the Santa Fe Trail been a national historic trail?
9 years in 1996

Flags over the Trail

Santa Fe, Spain . . . Mexico . . . USA. Land along the Santa Fe Trail has changed hands over the years. These modern flags represent nine countries and states that have owned or claimed territory along the Trail since 1820. Identify each flag. (Names are missing from two of the flags.)

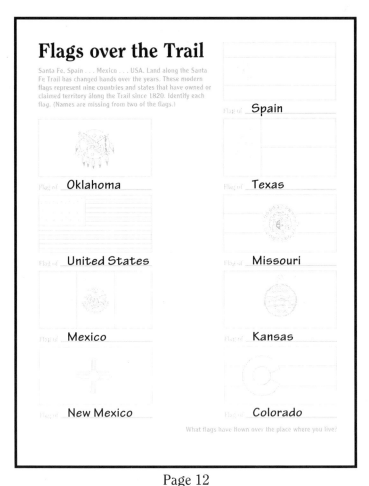

Flag of **Spain**
Flag of **Oklahoma**
Flag of **Texas**
Flag of **United States**
Flag of **Missouri**
Flag of **Mexico**
Flag of **Kansas**
Flag of **New Mexico**
Flag of **Colorado**

What flags have flown over the place where you live?

¿Habla usted español?

Do you speak Spanish? Even if you don't, you probably understand several Spanish words. That's because many words in Spanish and English come from the same Latin roots. And, over the years, cultural links like the Santa Fe Trail have helped blend the two languages. Use Spanish words from this list to complete the paragraph below.

Recently my family visited Santa Fe. At the [town square] **plaza** we saw a monument that marked the end of the Trail. At a nearby [restaurant] **café** I ordered a [meat and peppers rolled in cornmeal and cooked in a cornhusk] **tamale**. ["Thank you."] **Gracias** I told the waiter as he served me. That night, we were invited to a [celebration] **fiesta**. All the children were asked to help break a [clay or paper-mâché figure stuffed with candy and toys] **piñata**. When all the treats showered down, I was so excited my [mom] **mamá** said I was acting [wild or crazy] **loco**. The next day we went to Taos and toured an Indian [dwelling made of adobe and often in levels] **pueblo**. My [dad] **papá** bought a broad-brimmed hat [**sombrero**] as a souvenir. He yelled ["hurray"] **olé** as he pretended to be a bullfighter fighting a [bull] **toro**. When our trip was over, I hated to say [goodbye] **adiós** to New Mexico.

What other Spanish words in the list do you know?

Mile after mile

From what trailhead did Gregg measure?
Independence

Did his table follow the Cimarron Route or the Mountain Route?
Cimarron Route

State line traders crossed after 37 miles?
Missouri [Kansas]

According to the table, how far was 110-Mile Creek from the beginning?
95 miles

If traders moved 15 miles a day, how far would they have gone after 6 days?
90 miles

At that same rate, what stream would they have reached after 37 days?
McNees Creek

If wagons left Council Grove early on a Monday traveling 15 miles a day, what evening would they reach Lost Spring?
Tuesday evening

What point was almost halfway between Independence and Santa Fe?
Cimarron Crossing

How many miles followed the Arkansas?
122 miles

Traders often found no water from the time they left the Arkansas until they reached the Cimarron. How many miles?
58 miles

Find the mileage between Wagon Mound and Pawnee Rock.
364 miles

Miles between Cold Spring and Santa Fe?
240 miles

How many days were needed to travel from Cold Spring to Santa Fe?
16 days

Mystery map

1. Santa Fe
2. San Miguel
3. Fort Union
4. Wagon Mound
5. Raton Pass
6. Rabbit Ears
7. Camp Nichols
8. Cimarron River
9. Bent's Fort
10. Mountain Route
11. Chouteau's Island
12. Cimarron Route
13. Fort Dodge
14. Fort Larned
15. Pawnee Rock
16. Arkansas River
17. Council Grove
18. Fort Leavenworth
19. Fort Osage
20. Missouri River
21. Franklin

Mariano Yrissarri's bill of goods

Mariano Yrissarri, a merchant in Albuquerque, often traveled the Santa Fe Trail to buy goods in Missouri. The list at right contains just a few of the items he bought in St. Louis in 1853. Use prices from the list to complete the invoice below. Note: In many cases, Mariano purchased goods priced by the dozen. Here, most prices are listed per item.

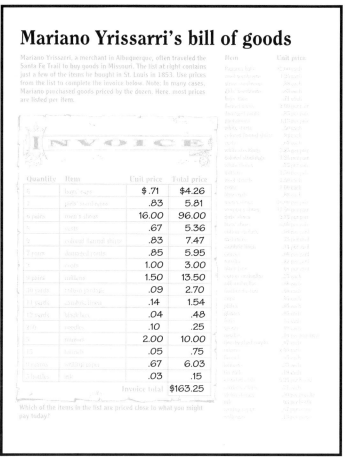

Which of the items in the list are priced close to what you might pay today?

Page 28

Josiah Gregg's graphs

Josiah Gregg made several trips to Santa Fe as a trader in the 1830s. The figures at right are from *Commerce of the Prairies*, a book he wrote in 1844 about the Santa Fe Trail. Use Gregg's table to complete the graphs showing Trail traffic over the years.

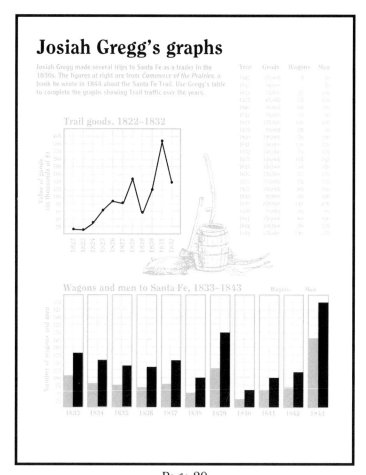

Page 29

J.J. Webb's puzzling list

The 33 bold items below are in the puzzle.

hairpins
hickory shirts
buck gloves
thread
brass nails
rings
pins
shawls
straps
blue denims
coffee mills
hooks
needles
spades
cork inkstands
black silk
necklaces
percussion caps
white cotton hose
pearl shirt buttons
padlocks
silk ties
bonnet ribbons
drawers
shovels
log chains
vest buttons
Irish linens

French lawns
tacks
satin jeans
butcher knives
ivory combs
razors
candlewick
suspenders
axes
beads
drillings
soap
scissors
pocket knives
muslins
saw files
sadirons
cambric
prints
vest buttons
needles/pins
calicoes
pongee
cambric
alpaca
cashmere
hoes
sadirons

Page 30

Webb's items

Dry goods
shawls
hickory shirts
buck gloves
blue denims
black silk
silk ties
flannel
Irish linens
French lawns
satin jeans
suspenders
drillings
muslins
prints
cambric
alpaca
cashmere
handkerchiefs
calicoes
pongee
cotton hose

Sewing notions
cotton thread
pins
hooks & eyes
needles
bonnet ribbons
coat buttons
vest buttons

Hardware
brass nails
axes
spades
padlocks
shovels
log chains
tacks
saw files
knives
iron spoons
sadirons
hoes

Jewelry
gold rings
beads
necklaces
ivory combs
hairpins

Miscellaneous
percussion caps
razor straps
cork inkstands
soap
candlewick

Page 31

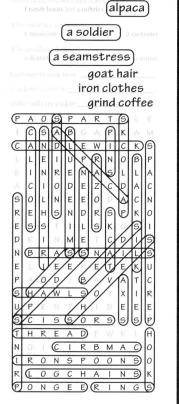

Page 35

Bosses, herders

I. Trail bosses
　A. Wagonmaster
　　1. One man per caravan
　　2. __In charge and made rules__
　　3. __Rode ahead of caravan__
　　4. __Chose campsites and route__
　　5. __Picked stream crossings__
　　6. __Scouted for Indians__
　　7. __Earned about $150 a month__
　B. Assistant wagonmaster
　　1. One man per caravan
　　2. Earned about $85 a month
　　3. __Kept slow wagons moving__
　　4. __Helped greenhorns__
　　5. __Rode near end of train__
II. Teamsters
　A. Bullwhackers
　　1. One man per wagon
　　2. Drove oxen
　　3. Earned about $50 a month
　　4. __Carried a five-pound whip__
　B. Mule skinners
　　1. __One man per wagon__
　　2. __Drove mules__
　　3. __Earned about $75 a month__
III. Other men
　A. Herders
　　1. Earned about $30 a month
　　2. __Two daytime, one night__
　　3. Took care of extra stock
　B. Extra hands
　　1. Earned about $30 a month
　　2. __Three or four per caravan__
　　3. __Replaced deserters or sick__

Page 36

A long day

An ordinary day on the Santa Fe Trail was hard work for travelers and animals. Number these statements about a typical Trail day in the correct order. Use information from "On the march" (page 37) to help.

__8__ If necessary, the wagons crossed a stream before stopping to make camp.

__2__ Crews rounded up animals, sorted, and hitched them to begin the morning.

__9__ Before the men ate their evening meal, they unhitched teams and took care of the animals.

__1__ The cook or night herder woke the men.

__10__ After their meal, the men made repairs before they relaxed around the campfire.

__6__ After eating, the men repaired wagons and harnesses, doctored animals, hunted, or did other necessary work.

__7__ The animals were rehitched and the caravan traveled several more hours.

__3__ About 10 A.M., the train stopped for a midday rest.

__11__ Most men bedded down while the night herders stayed awake.

__4__ Men unhitched teams at midday to let the animals drink, graze, and rest.

__5__ The cook served the men their biggest meal of the day.

Page 40

Wheelers, leaders, pointers

Whether using oxen or mules, traders hitched their teams in the same pattern. Use the bold words in the sentences below to complete these diagrams.

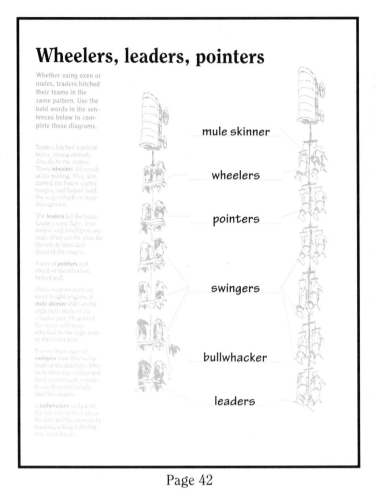

mule skinner
wheelers
pointers
swingers
bullwhacker
leaders

Page 42

Spans of mules—or yokes of oxen?

Santa Fe traders faced a decision—which animals should pull their wagons. Use "A choice: mules or oxen" (page 41) to list some advantages and disadvantages of using both kinds of animals on the Trail.

Advantages	Advantages
• Stronger than horses	• Cheaper than mules
• Ate less than horses	• Needed less feed
• Longer working lives than horses	• Could graze off grass
• Fewer saddle sores than horses	• Yokes cheaper than harnesses
• Could be trained in a short time	• Hoofs pulled well
• [Pulled faster than oxen]	• Meat could be eaten
	• Did not appeal to Indians

Disadvantages	Disadvantages
• Expensive	• Pulled slower than mules
• Harnesses, singletrees and doubletrees were expensive	• Hoofs became tender
• Temperamental [stubborn, easily stampeded, kicked]	• Sometimes got sick from poisonous plants or cattle diseases
• [Needed extra feed]	• Did not work well in very hot weather
• [Hoofs didn't pull well through mud and sand]	• Sometimes didn't survive very cold weather
• [Not usually eaten]	
• [Indians sometimes stole]	

	1840s	1860s		1840s	1860s
One span of average-priced mules = $	300	750	One yoke of average-priced oxen = $	25	150
One team (8 spans) = $	1,800	4,500	One team (6 yokes) = $	150	900
One average-sized caravan (26 teams) = $	46,800	117,000	One average-sized caravan (26 teams) = $	3,900	23,400
			Cost difference between wagon trains of mules and wagon trains of oxen = $	42,900	93,600

Page 43

Trail schooner

Wagons built for use on the Santa Fe Trail had to stand up to rugged use. Although many of their parts were wooden (to save weight), most Trail wagons could carry 4,000 pounds or more. Match the bold words in the clues below with the missing labels on the wagon diagram.

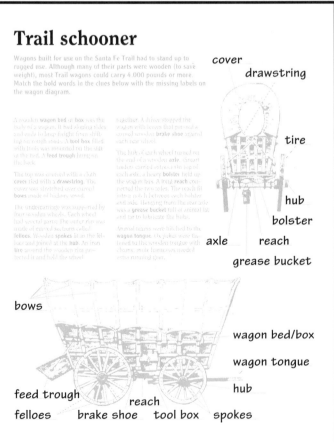

cover
drawstring
tire
hub
bolster
axle reach
grease bucket

bows
wagon bed/box
wagon tongue
hub
feed trough reach
felloes brake shoe tool box spokes

Page 45

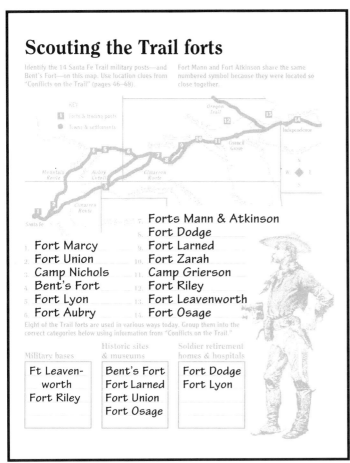
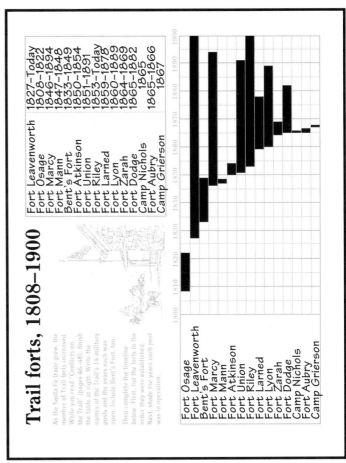
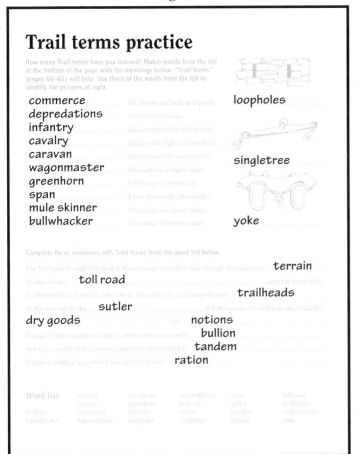
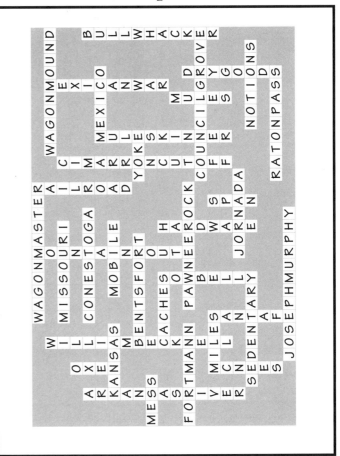

Page 64

Name	Year	Place		Year Place
Francis X. Aubry [pg 8]	1824	Quebec Canada	1846 as a trader	1854 Santa Fe NM
William Bent [pg 18]	1809	St. Louis Missouri	1829 as a trader with his brother	1869 Colorado
"Kit" Carson [pg 18]	1809	Kentucky	1826 as a runaway working as a herder	1868 Fort Lyon Colorado
Antonio José Chávez [pg 16]	1810	New Mexico	probably with his trading family or as a trader	1843 KS [Chávez Creek]
Mary Donoho [pg 39]	1807	Tennessee	1833 with her husband	1880 Texas
Ernestine Huning [pg 50]	1837 or '38	Bavaria	1863 with her trader husband	1923 Albuquerque NM
Franz Huning [pg 50]	1827	Germany	1849 as a bullwhacker	1905 Albuquerque NM
Little Raven [pg 50]	about 1817	about Nebraska	? grew up in Trail country	1889 Cantonment OK
Susan Magoffin [pg 51]	1827	Kentucky	1846 with her trader husband	1855 Missouri
Alexander Majors [pg 39]	1814	Kentucky	1848 as a trader	1900 Chicago Illinois
"Buffalo Bill" Mathewson [pg 33]	1830	New York	by 1852 probably as an Indian trader or trapper	1916 Wichita Kansas
"Lissie" Mathewson [pg 17]	1842	England	1864 with her trader husband	1885 Wichita Kansas
Marion Russell [pg 17]	1845	Illinois	1852 with her mother	1936 Trinidad Colorado
Robert Wright [pg 34]	1840	Maryland	1859 as a bullwhacker	1915 Dodge City KS

Page 65

Quick quiz

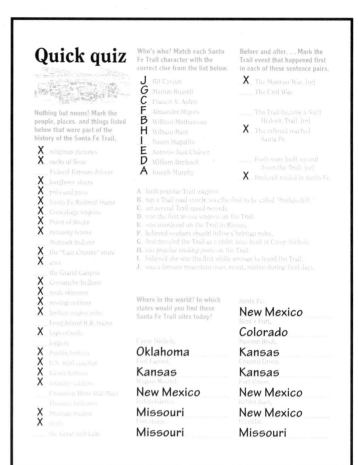

Nothing but nouns! Mark the people, places, and things listed below that were part of the history of the Santa Fe Trail.

- X religious pictures
- X sacks of flour
- _ Federal Express drivers
- _ longhorn steers
- X pots and pans
- _ Santa Fe Railroad trains
- X Conestoga wagons
- _ Point of Rocks
- X runaway teams
- _ Mohawk Indians
- _ the "Last Chance" store
- X axes
- _ the Grand Canyon
- X Comanche Indians
- X mule skinners
- X sewing notions
- _ broken wagon axles
- _ Long Island R.R. trains
- X kegs of nails
- _ loafers
- X Pueblo Indians
- _ U.S. mail coaches
- X Kiowa Indians
- _ infantry soldiers
- _ Cimarron River Wal-Mart
- _ Thomas Jefferson
- X Mexican traders
- X cloth
- _ the Great Salt Lake

Who's who? Match each Santa Fe Trail character with the correct clue from the list below.

- J Kit Carson
- G Marion Russell
- C Francis X. Aubry
- F Alexander Majors
- B William Mathewson
- H William Bent
- I Susan Magoffin
- E Antonio José Chávez
- D William Becknell
- A Joseph Murphy

A. built popular Trail wagons.
B. ran a Trail road ranch; was the first to be called "Buffalo Bill".
C. set several Trail speed records.
D. was the first to use wagons on the Trail.
E. was murdered on the Trail in Kansas.
F. believed workers should follow Christian rules.
G. first traveled the Trail as a child; later lived at Camp Nichols.
H. ran popular trading posts on the Trail.
I. believed she was the first white woman to travel the Trail.
J. was a famous mountain man, scout, soldier during Trail days.

Before and after... Mark the Trail event that happened first in each of these sentence pairs.

- X The Mexican War, [or]
- _ The Civil War.

- _ The Trail became a Nat'l Historic Trail, [or]
- X The railroad reached Santa Fe.

- _ Forts were built up and down the Trail, [or]
- X Becknell traded in Santa Fe.

Where in the world? In which states would you find these Santa Fe Trail sites today?

Santa Fe	New Mexico
Bent's Fort	Colorado
Camp Nichols	Oklahoma
Pawnee Rock	Kansas
Fort Larned	Kansas
Council Grove	Kansas
Wagon Mound	New Mexico
Fort Union	New Mexico
Independence	Missouri
Rabbit Ears	New Mexico
Fort Leavenworth	Missouri
Franklin	Missouri

Page 66

Trail review

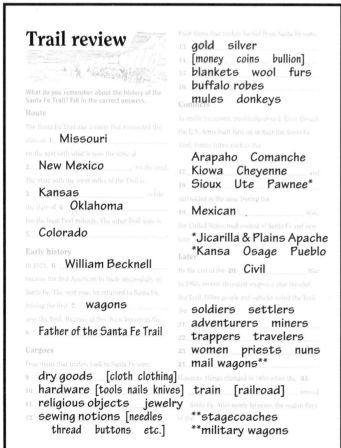

What do you remember about the history of the Santa Fe Trail? Fill in the correct answers.

Route

The Santa Fe Trail was a route that connected the state of 1. **Missouri** on the east with what is now the state of 2. **New Mexico** on the west. The state with the most miles of the Trail is 3. **Kansas**, while the state of 4. **Oklahoma** has the least Trail mileage. The other Trail state is 5. **Colorado**.

Early history

In 1821, 6. **William Becknell** became the first American to trade successfully in Santa Fe. The next year, he returned to Santa Fe, driving the first 7. **wagons** over the Trail. Because of this, he is known as the 8. **Father of the Santa Fe Trail**.

Cargoes

Four items that traders took to Santa Fe were:
9. **dry goods** [cloth clothing]
10. **hardware** [tools nails knives]
11. **religious objects** jewelry
12. **sewing notions** [needles thread buttons etc.]

Four items that traders hauled from Santa Fe were:
13. **gold silver** [money coins bullion]
15. **blankets wool furs**
16. **buffalo robes**
    mules donkeys

Conflicts

As traffic increased, trouble developed. Even though the U.S. Army built forts on or near the Santa Fe Trail, Indian tribes such as the **Arapaho Comanche Kiowa Cheyenne** and 17/18. **Sioux Ute Pawnee*** still raided in the area. During the 19. **Mexican** War, the United States took control of Santa Fe and new *Jicarilla & Plains Apache **Kansa Osage Pueblo** Later, by the end of the 20. **Civil** War in 1865, several thousand wagons a year traveled the Trail. Other people and vehicles using the Trail were **soldiers settlers** 21. **adventurers miners** 22. **trappers travelers** 23. **women priests nuns** 24. **mail wagons**** However, things changed in 1880 when the 25. **train [railroad]** arrived in Santa Fe. After nearly 60 years, the wagon days of the **stagecoaches** **military wagons** were over.

Page 67

Match these Santa Fe Trail characters, places, and terms with the correct definitions.

- G Kit Carson
- M caravan
- K mule skinner
- J Fort Union
- F Pawnee Rock
- H William Bent
- N commerce
- C bullwhacker
- E Fort Leavenworth
- A Conestoga
- B Wagon Mound
- O Bent's Fort

A. a popular Trail wagon made in Pennsylvania
B. a famous New Mexican Trail landmark
C. an ox driver
D. a wagon builder in St. Louis
E. a fort/fort near the Trail that is still an active U.S. Army base
F. a famous Kansas Trail landmark
G. was known along the Trail as a scout, soldier, and mountain man
H. ran popular trading posts on the Trail
I. took the first wagons over the Trail
J. an important Trail fort in New Mexico with a large supply depot
K. a mule driver
L. a fort along the Cimarron River
M. a group of traders and their wagons traveling together
N. the buying and selling of goods
O. an important trading post on the Trail

Match these names with the numbers on the Trail map.

- 21 Missouri River
- 15 Arkansas River
- 17 Oregon Trail
- 25 Missouri
- 8 Aubry Cutoff
- 3 Santa Fe
- 1 Colorado
- 2 New Mexico
- 20 Fort Dodge
- 16 Council Grove
- 11 Cimarron Route
- 22 Franklin
- 12 Cimarron River
- 5 Wagon Mound
- 13 Fort Larned
- 14 Pawnee Rock
- 4 Fort Union
- 24 Oklahoma
- 7 Camp Nichols
- 9 Bent's Fort
- 23 Kansas
- 10 Mountain Route
- 19 Independence
- 18 Fort Leavenworth
- 6 Raton Pass

KEY
1. Landmarks
2. Forts & trading posts
3. Towns & settlements
4. Trails, rivers & states